NEW
UNITED

About the Author

Denis Cassidy grew up in a working-class district of Newcastle-upon-Tyne in the 1930s and '40s. He watched his first match at St James' Park in 1943 and began work as an office junior in Newcastle in 1949.

A varied career in business led to his appointment to the Board of British Home Stores in the 1970s, followed by his appointment as Managing Director in the 1980s. He went on to take Directorships at BAA, SEEBOARD, Compass Group and Forever Broadcasting, as well as many Chairmanships, including Bhs, Boddingtons, Liberty, Ferguson International, and Newcastle United.

Denis is a Fellow of the Royal Society of Arts and an author. His first book *The Way Things Were – A Backstreet Boyhood* was published in 2005, and is set in Newcastle. Sir Bobby Robson contributed a foreword to the book.

NEWCASTLE UNITED

THE DAY THE PROMISES HAD TO STOP

DENIS CASSIDY

AMBERLEY

This book is dedicated to the memory of my father, Harry, and my brothers, Alan, Vincent, Rex and Sydney, with whom I shared my love of football and Newcastle United on the terraces of St James' Park

This revised edition first published 2012
First published 2010

Amberley Publishing
The Hill, Stroud
Gloucestershire, GL5 4EP

www.amberleybooks.com

British Library Cataloguing in Publication Data.
A catalogue record for this book is available from the British Library.

ISBN 978 1 4456 0903 4

Typesetting and Origination by Amberley Publishing.
Printed in Great Britain.

Contents

Preface

The first edition was published in June 2010. The theme of the book was to use the recent history of one club to illustrate the impact of and responses to the changes which had been triggered by the creation of the English Premier League. Some of these changes have been seen as beneficial while others have sent shock waves through the English, European and International Football governance structures. The introduction of Financial Fair Play rules and the continuing debate on goal line technology are only two obvious examples. The damage wrought to some clubs by a reckless pursuit of the riches and prestige of winning the Premiership has caused the demise of many well known, some famous, clubs. Similarly the cost to a club of a single simple error by a match official can be, and has been, hugely disproportionate when that has resulted in relegation or the loss of an important game as direct result.

Football by its very nature produces very different results every season and because of this I have updated the 2010 first edition by adding additional chapters to cover the results of the last 2 seasons. This is important as the club I chose to illustrate the impact of the creation of the Premiership was Newcastle United and to use that to reveal how the ambitions and motives of owners and managers create pressures and pitfalls in their pursuit of glory and potential riches. Using Newcastle United as a metaphor was and remains an apt choice.

The evidence of the last 2 seasons also serves to emphasise the conclusions set out in the first edition – that most of the clubs which have failed in the Premiership could have reduced or avoided the cost of failure by an intelligent, objective appreciation of their prospects for survival. In many cases such an unsuccessful period in the Premiership has resulted in bankruptcy and/or change of ownership. The same objective analysis reveals, of course, which clubs are most likely to prosper and which have, by deduction, been the obvious underperformers.

I hope that fans, owners, and managers alike may benefit from a better understanding of these issues and that it is a gateway to deriving even more enjoyment from this wonderful game.

Now we can all look forward to the 2012/13 season and beyond.

Denis Cassidy
May 2012

Introduction

Football has been a major part of my life since I was old enough to walk and kick a ball. And at the age of ten, after watching my first professional football game, I fell under the spell of Newcastle United. However, that passion, born in me and nurtured by growing up in that great city, led to an interest in and a love for the game as a whole.

As with so many other elements of our daily lives, the pace of change has increased dramatically in the last twenty years and that pattern is set to continue. For football fans throughout the UK and indeed beyond our shores, the creation of the Premier League in 1992 has probably had the most profound impact on the professional game, bringing more changes, many unforeseen and some unwelcome, than previously experienced in its 130-year history.

This story is about the Premier League's impact on the game as a whole and how players, managers, directors, owners, regulators, and supporters of all clubs have been affected. I have chosen to do this by telling the story of my club, Newcastle United, but in so doing I believe all supporters of every club, regardless of league or position, will see in this tale something of their own club and their own lives.

It is a story of high achievement in a long and glorious history, of broken promises, and of unnecessary failure through incompetence, greed, and vanity. In short, a tragedy that in today's world should be portrayed as the abuse of innocent victims. Victims? Yes, not one but several: the city, the club, the local culture, and above all the loyal supporters who return year after year after year, praying and longing for success. Yet it is the fans' craving for success and reluctance to acknowledge the risks inherent in attracting the serious money needed to satisfy those ambitions that has played the major role in both the triumphs and the tragedies.

This story is one of the tragedies – but that may be about to change. As I wrote this book, the team won the Championship without losing a single home game, and will return to the Premiership in 2010/11. Is this just another false dawn, or a glorious rebirth?

Once a supporter, always a supporter. In short, think of the Newcastle United of this recent era as a metaphor for all clubs. Enjoy it, digest it. Here's to a successful 2010/11 season for whatever team you support, in whatever league it plays.

Denis Cassidy
June 2010

1

Relegation, and a Conversation with Myself, May 2009

It was just after 6.15 p.m. on Saturday 24 May 2009, a gloriously sunny late spring evening, and I sat in a melancholy trance listening sadly to the predictable words of regret falling from the mouths of the sad-faced professionals who had failed in their allotted tasks. They were all managers of Premiership football teams, two of which were now relegated to the lower Championship Division. For their club, the financial consequence would be a reduction in income of tens of millions of pounds, but that pales into insignificance in the minds of the thousands of supporters when ranked with their sense of loss, the crushing of their dreams, and the futility of a season wasted. Some will never have experienced relegation before; others, like me, have done so many times, and yet it feels worse – it really is worse – this time.

How can that be so?
Because my team is Newcastle United and it has just been relegated from the Premiership, the richest, the most international, and the most prestigious league in the world.

But other teams have been relegated and bounced back, why the gloom?
Because Newcastle was made for the Premiership. The league was designed by the top English clubs for themselves, to enable them to prosper – and its history confirms that it is one of those top clubs.

I still don't get it, just rebuild and reclaim your rightful place! Why the angst?
Listen carefully and I shall tell you why I am so committed to this club. I will also tell you in detail the significance of today and its link to a similar day seventeen years ago. I will repeat what you know already, how that led to discovery of the formula for success in the Premiership, of how that

formula was discarded, of the people who could have made Newcastle's success permanent, and of those whose profligacy I feel was responsible for the catastrophe we see today!

OK! I am listening. To make sure I really understand this time, leave nothing out. Please finish on an optimistic note. Being gloomy doesn't sit well with you and Newcastle United, does it?
I know what needs to be done and how it can be achieved, but I can't control events. I think Mr Ashley has given up, accepts he has made terrible errors and will sell to anybody – well, almost anybody – who will put up the cash. Not an easy task in 2009, and there is no guarantee that whoever buys it will understand the issues any better than he or his immediate predecessors: Sir John Hall, Douglas Hall, and Freddy Shepherd.

You're getting pessimistic again and this is no time for pessimism! A solution is required urgently. So get on with it. Somebody is bound to see the opportunity to rejoice in the resurrection of this great club.
But that's what we all thought would happen when John Hall acquired the club, and again when Mike Ashley paid a lot of money to buy it from the Halls and the Shepherds only two years ago! It is not sufficient to say, 'Of course, they will understand!'

Enough of this navel gazing, just tell me the story – you've already told me you will leave nothing out.
OK. Let me start by highlighting what I regard as the points of crisis and opportunity that have occurred in the last twenty years, by repeating the words used publicly at the time, plus some made privately in conversation with me, and which I have never told anyone about until now.

Sounds fine to me – off you go.
Good.

- **John Hall, 1984, in a private conversation, before he displayed any interest in NUFC:** 'I am not a Newcastle supporter, if anything I was a Sunderland fan.'

- **John Hall, 1988, in the published document 'A Pledge for the Future' in The Magpie Group Charter:** 'To revitalise the Board, to inject up to £5 million of new cash into the club, to democratise the Club.'

- **John Hall, 1991, on being appointed Chairman of NUFC:** 'I never wanted this job anyway.'

- **Cameron Hall Developments' formal announcement, 1992:** 'Newcastle United is now a wholly owned subsidary of Cameron Hall Developments Ltd.'

- **John Hall, 1996, in a private conversation the morning after the 0-1 home defeat against Manchester United:** 'It's a complete disaster, a total disaster, we've blown it and I told Kevin so last night.'

- **Kevin Keegan, May 1996, in a Newcastle United match programme:** 'I will be desperately disappointed if we're runners up, because I believed from day one that we could be Champions.'

- **John Hall, in the same programme:** 'We have always known that the psychological barrier we have to break is to win something.'

- **Kevin Keegan to *The Times*, October 1996, after beating Manchester United 5-0:** 'I awoke yesterday to criticism, some of it from top people, about the way we are doing it. We opened up today, we played *our* way. We proved the League can be won by attacking football.'

- **Australian radio announcement, January 1997:** 'We are going over to the UK for news of a shock resignation – *pause* – a story of a resignation which has shaken the football world to its foundations has just been announced, Kevin Keegan has resigned as Manager of Newcastle United.'

- *News of the World* **front page, 15 March 1998:** 'VICE GIRLS SHAME OF TOP SOCCER BOSSES' (Remarks recorded and repeated in article include Douglas Hall and Freddy Shepherd's description of the fans as 'mugs', the women of Newcastle as 'all dogs', and Alan Shearer as like 'Mary Poppins'.)

- **Freddy Shepherd, 1998, on being told he must resign:** 'Don't f*****g moralise at me.'

- **In a formal apology to fans prior to rejoining the Football Club Board, Shepherd refers to the scandal as** 'the controversial issue in March'.

- **Shepherd in the match programme for first home game of the 1998/99 season:** 'It is not my intention to dwell on the unhappy incident in March.' **There was also a reminder of** 'our deep seated love for this club and our respect and admiration for the people who support it'. **His stated intention** was to 'back Kenny Dalglish every step of the way'. Dalglish was said to have resigned three days later.

- **The announcement to the London Stock Exchange of BSkyB's bid to acquire Manchester United in September 1998.**

- **Announcement by the Board of Newcastle United, 8 December 1998:** 'The Board announces the appointment of Douglas Hall and Freddy Shepherd to the (PLC) Board with immediate effect. The Company also announces that Denis Cassidy, John Josephs and Tom Fenton felt they could not continue in such circumstances.'

- **NUFC announcement, December 1998:** 'The Board ... announces that NTL Inc. ... has entered into an agreement with Cameron Hall Developments LTD ... to acquire 9,000,000 shares [representing 6.3% of the issued share capital of NUFC] at a price of 111.7p per share ... Cameron Hall has also entered into an irrevocable commitment with NTL ... to accept an offer [for] the balance [of their shares] equal to a further 50.8% of the PLC shares in issue.'

- **Extract from the Wembley FA Cup semi-final programme, April 2000:** 'If the Newcastle United story of 1999/2000 had been broadcast as a soap opera, East Enders and Coronation Street would have lost out in the ratings war.'

- **Sir Bobby Robson, August 2004, in a private conversation with me:** 'But why do they want me to go, Denis? We've finished 3rd, 4th, and 5th in the last three years.'

- **Freddy Shepherd, September 2004, in a match programme:** 'Sir Bobby and I parted on very good terms. We had some great times together.'

- **Freddy Shepherd, January 2005:** 'Many of the problems Graeme [Souness] has faced are down to the way the previous Manager handled discipline.'

- **Sir John Hall, 2005, interviewed on TV:** 'He [Sir Bobby] should have been sacked after the Marseille game.'

- **Douglas Hall, 2005, in an interview with the *Daily Mirror*:** 'We had to get rid of Sir Bobby Robson because he would have got us relegated.'

- **Announcement to the stock exchange, May 2007:** 'SJHL, a company owned and controlled by Mike Ashley, has bought 55,342,223 shares in the company, Newcastle United PLC, representing 41.6% of its issued share capital.'

- **Announcement to the stock exchange, June 2007:** 'SJHL and the company, Newcastle United PLC, have reached agreement on the terms of a recommended offer for the entire issued and to be issued share capital not already held by SJHL.'

- **Announcement by Mike Ashley, September 2008:** 'I have listened to you. You want me out. That is what I am now trying to do.'

- **Sir Bobby Robson, May 2009, in a private conversation with me:** 'Denis, if you had still been Chairman, me the Manager and Freddie [Fletcher] Chief Executive this would never have happened.'

In May 2009, Newcastle United was relegated from the Premiership to the Championship. It's clear from this summary that everyone who loves the club should take heed, and not just of those who share a passion for Newcastle. What follows is the full story, the highs *and* the lows, but who knows what's next? Tomorrow is another day.

2

A Great Club is Born

I believe there are three major categories of football fans and that each has its defining characteristics.

The first is one who has been born into a family or in a town or city where allegiance to the local club is as much a way of life as the religion the family practises or the dialect they speak. In reality, you don't choose your club; it adopts you as one of its followers.

The second is the fan who adopts a club, usually because it is successful at the time they first take a serious interest in the game or because they have moved to a city where a football ground is accessible.

The third is the fan who adopts a club for social or business reasons. I include some major shareholders and owners in this category.

As I shall explain, I belong to the first group. While I welcome all genuine fans, only the first group has the distinguishing characteristics of unswerving loyalty and devotion that matches the qualities of an enduring love affair.

The third group is pragmatic and susceptible to fads, fashion, ego, or greed. The second group of fans can have characteristics of either of the other groups – their conversion might be permanent, or a passing fad.

I was born in 1933 into a family dominated by boys. We lived in a small overcrowded flat in a working class district of Newcastle a few minutes' walk from St James' Park and I became a fan as inevitably as had my father.

Football was only one of the games developed in Britain during the Industrial Revolution, but it was more obviously shaped by the cramped conditions of nineteenth-century urban living than any other. Small houses, large families, little money, and children's inexhaustible need for inexpensive play were the seeds from which it grew. A back lane between terraces of small houses and flats provided the pitch and endless back lane walls were used as touch lines. If a ball was unavailable, a bundle of rags or a stone could be substituted. Life itself was a contest for survival and bred a spirit of competitiveness manifested in the creation of local teams.

Teams gave rise to organised leagues and in 1888 the Football League was formed, dominated by teams from the industrial heartlands of the North and the Midlands. But at the time, Newcastle neither sought nor was invited to join.

My father was born in May 1892, the year that Newcastle United was formed by a merger of Newcastle West End and Newcastle East End. The former had a deepening financial crisis brought about by poor performances on the field, declining gates, and the cost burden of the newly acquired pitch, St James' Park; the East End brought a stronger team with better management and a need for a better ground.

This history seems, with the retrospective wisdom of a century's experience, to more closely resemble a witch's curse. Both teams were members of the Northern League but now sought membership of the Football League created four years earlier, of which Sunderland were the new Champions. The application, by the newly formed Newcastle United, was rejected. The club was offered membership of the new Second Division, which was declined. A year later, Newcastle applied again and got the same response, an offer of membership of the lower division, which this time was accepted. Along with Liverpool, Middlesbrough, and Woolwich Arsenal, Newcastle joined the Second Division. By the end of the 1898/99 season, Newcastle had won promotion to the First Division and started a run of improving results, culminating in their first golden period, from the 1903/04 season to 1914, when competition was halted by the First World War. They finished in the top four in nine of the 11 seasons, winning the First Division title in three years of a five-year period and winning one of five FA Cup Finals in which they appeared. It was a very promising and exciting first twenty years in the Football League.

Little wonder that my father was captivated by United then and throughout his life. He married in 1916 and together with my mother seemed to weave their married life with that of United. He took a job as a tram conductor and through that regularly met and chatted with his idols, the great players of the inter-war years, who daily travelled on trams to and from the ground during the season.

My eldest brother Alan was born in 1924 when Newcastle won the FA Cup for the second time. Vincent was born in 1927, the year they last won the First Division title. Rex was born in 1930, a year distinguished by the crash of the Airship R101. I was born when Newcastle were holders of the Cup again, having beaten Arsenal the previous year. By the time the youngest, Sydney, was born, Newcastle had been relegated to the Second Division, where they were to remain throughout the Second World War.

During the early years of the war, my father, 'Pop' as we knew him, frequently regaled the boys with stories of Newcastle's great deeds and individual heroes, many of whom he would describe, with a touch of Bass Bitter-induced hyperbole, as 'old friends'. This constant informal diet of football history fed into our back lane games. The process continued through primary school until, in 1943, when competitive football was resumed in the UK on a local league basis, I made my first visit to St James' Park, saw United win 5-2, had the first sight of my own heroes Albert Stubbins and Jackie Milburn, and was hooked forever.

Everything thereafter was subordinated to a desire to see them play as often as possible and in our school or back lane games we all sought to replicate their skills and mannerisms. Weekends were dominated by school, back lane and street team matches or, in a quasi-professional way, on Sundays on the Town Moor against any happy bunch of pre-lunch drinkers on their way home. They readily paid a small fee to join in our game, seeking to re-enact the game they had watched the previous afternoon. In truth we timed our arrival as a spider spins its web, but all in a good cause: to fund another visit to St James'.

Then, as the final years of war gave way to peace, United enjoyed a renaissance as it planned, acquired, shaped, and continually refreshed a great side. Football fans throughout the country enjoyed their compelling and attractive brand of football. This team, built around an entertaining 'attacking' vision, was studded with prolific goal-scoring forwards such as Stubbins (232 goals including 29 hat-tricks), Milburn (238 goals in 353 appearances) and many others, including Bentley, Shackleton (6 goals in his debut), Robledo, White, Wayman, and Mitchell.

It was no surprise when promotion from the Second Division followed in May 1948. The team were runners-up, but had the most wins and highest number of goals scored in the division. The attacking style of football led to 3 FA Cup wins in five years of the 1950s, but the team couldn't achieve better than 4th place in the First Division. However, from the mid-1950s, attendance declined progressively from an average of over 56,000 on promotion to less than 27,000 as the team slipped down the table. They were relegated to the Second Division in 1961, despite scoring 86 goals in the same season. By then, I had moved away from Newcastle, as some seasons of flickering promise, alternating with patent failure, followed. The outlook was depressing, thanks to the Board's inability to manage the club's finances, a lacklustre team, a decaying Victorian stadium, disputes with the local council over redevelopment plans, and a payroll set to increase following the abolition of players' maximum wage of £20 per week.

As the years passed, a frustrated fan base, more affluent than at any time in the club's history, watched their dreams of glory crushed, but this time they were more keenly aware of what they had lost and desperately wished to regain. The fans were filled with ambition and hungry for success – for which they were prepared and able to pay.

For me, a glorious period lasting continuously for almost twenty years now came to an end. It was marked, as my father's had been at the beginning of the century, by exuberant, stylish football, studded with trophies won by legendary players lavished with widespread affection. A store of wonderful memories had been created by the excitement and joy of those days. How can you forget being part of a crowd of over 66,000 people straining every nerve, suffering every moment of stress, until the final whistle blows, and only then do you know that you have collectively done it – secured promotion to the First Division with a nail-biting last surge and a 4-2 victory? Or the pride of going to your first FA Cup Final, of being stopped and encouraged by a Guards officer in full ceremonial dress with the comment, 'howay the lads'?

This is the life of a fan in his schooldays. But schoolboys grow up, and the rest of this story is the view of a fan whose adult life began to weave itself into the developing drama of his team in a changing world. The ups and downs of the next twenty years were a replay of history – strife on and off the pitch, and a revolving door for managers, players, and directors, driven inevitably, but avoidably, by a lack of stability and an absence of strategy.

On completion of my first twenty years as a fan, the witch's curse had struck again, and it was to be another twenty years before there were any lasting signs of a possible return to the old days of glory. There were promising moments of resurgence with the European Fairs Cup win of 1969, and two (losing) Wembley appearances in the FA Cup of 1974 and the League Cup of 1976.

Relegated in 1961, promoted in 1965, almost relegated in 1967 – finishing 20th, having scored only 39 goals – and relegated yet again in 1978 after another decade of sinking slowly. A fundamental change was required, but who would be the catalyst? Two individuals were to influence the history, destiny, and success of Newcastle United for many years to come – Kevin Keegan and John Hall.

My role moved beyond that of fan as I met others who had played or were to play some part in the next glorious episode – Cardinal Hume, Jackie Milburn, Bobby Robson, Douglas Hall, Freddy Shepherd, and Freddie Fletcher.

One thing was clear; change for the better was overdue. Logic and history suggested that it would be by Geordies, for Geordies.

3

Two Geordie Pitmen
to the Rescue

It was through my expanding business roles that I found myself meeting for the first time virtually all of the men who were, eventually, to play major parts in the next phase of Newcastle United's history.

In 1980, as Sales Director of British Home Stores, I was responsible for all stores and all marketing activities. The company was in a period of strong growth and was actively seeking new store sites to expand the existing nationwide chain. We also wanted to strengthen our presence in markets such as children's wear, and it was through a combination of these two unlikely routes that I was drawn closer to those 'influencers in waiting'. Even though I had moved away from Tyneside in 1958, I had never lost touch with or ceased to watch United, because family, friends, and business activities provided regular opportunities for me to visit Newcastle and to watch a home game. When debating with colleagues the possibility of improving links with schools to improve their awareness of our 'Back to School' clothing ranges, some form of football sponsorship seemed to offer an attractive route. This led us to the English Schools Football Association and a meeting with the Secretary, who turned out to be yet another Geordie, Jim Robinson, a Headmaster from a Durham school who was a lifelong Newcastle supporter. The consequences were as impressive as they were rapid. We agreed to finance a county-based schools football competition and purchased a beautiful silver trophy – I still swear it was made from the original FA Cup, stolen in 1895. For our press briefing, we needed a leading football personality. 'No problem,' said Jim, and he produced his ace, the newly appointed England Manager, Bobby Robson. What a star Bobby was at the launch.

Afterwards we talked for a long time about his career and shared boyhood memories, hardly surprising since we were born in the same month of the same year and could swap tales of the glory days we both had enjoyed as schoolboys at St. James'. I reminded him of the day in 1951 when a rumour swept the North East that United had offered Fulham a huge sum for their three eighteen-year-old future stars – Haynes, Jezzard and Robson – but it had failed. That day was a precursor of success for Bobby as England Manager, for the football competition we launched, and for the personal contacts made which survived until his death in 2009. Our paths crossed many times over the years, as you will see.

Simultaneously, the Store Development team proposed we take a site in a planned out-of-town shopping centre to be built on the site of a disused, half-demolished power station at Dunston, Gateshead. I rejected the idea, as we already had a large, highly successful store in Newcastle city centre, and others elsewhere in the region. However, they pleaded that the planned centre would have a major impact on shopping habits in the North East. The fact that it was to be built by an unknown developer, John Hall, who had never built anything else previously on anything approaching this scale, did not lessen their enthusiasm. This only hardened my belief that this was so unlikely a proposition that it could not compete with other known priorities for available funds, and I again rejected it. However, Mr Hall was a persistent and tenacious advocate for his scheme, and before long I had been persuaded by my colleagues to go to Newcastle to meet him.

It was my first meeting with John Hall. He drove me from the station in his Jaguar to the site where, in the only building there, the site hut, we changed our shoes for Wellington boots, the minimum requirement to see a site which was a sea of mud with a huge pile of rubble in one corner, rather like a Second World War bomb site with which I was very familiar. There was nothing else to see and I knew I was right – I was wasting my time. John now exchanged the Jaguar for a mud-spattered Land Rover and we set off bumpily with nothing to see except some hand-painted signs mounted on fence posts, which variously declared 'Anchor Store', then more bumps, more mud, then another, 'Lake', then another, 'Food Store', and yet another, 'Hotel', at which I burst into uncontrolled laughter. John was not amused as I told him that this scene was lifted straight from *The Dandy* comic of our childhood, if he substituted Desperate Dan's 'cow town' for the Dunston site. I reminded John of this lasting impression often in years to come. After an unconvincing tour we drove to his house in Low Fell where I was given a tour of the site on paper in his 'Exhibition', a euphemism for his garage, and we had lunch which his wife Mae cooked, served, and cleared while John the passionate sought to persuade me to acquire a site in a non-stop monologue. He believed in the grand scheme, he knew he was right, and, however unlikely it seemed to me, it was going to happen.

The problem was that I remained unconvinced. I left, and he pursued me relentlessly in the months that followed, keen for me to change my mind and take a site. Minor retailers had already agreed terms and some small development was taking place.

Although I had outlined my reservations about the scheme's viability in general, and for British Home Stores in particular, I told him that if he could persuade Marks & Spencer, the high street superpower in those days, to participate, we would certainly follow swiftly. He did just that and so we followed. In the process, we got to know each other extremely well. Yet in all those conversations, he never even mentioned Newcastle United, although he did tell me he either was or had been a Sunderland supporter.

John, when focused on an objective, became obsessed with it and in this case he was right to do so. He proved all his doubters wrong, including me, and he deservedly made his fortune. He was to use his newfound wealth, his personality, and his influence to seize control of the perennially struggling Newcastle United, but that was still some years ahead.

Before that happened, my new-found ally, Jim Robinson, had been asked to help us out again. Our store in Northumberland Street, Newcastle, had been redesigned and we sought a Geordie personality to reopen it. What greater personality on Tyneside could we want but Wor Jackie? Jackie Milburn had been my hero since childhood, as he was for most Geordies, including His Eminence Cardinal Hume, with whom I agreed readily when he pronounced to me that Jackie was the greatest footballer he had ever seen.

Jim delivered again. We met Jackie for dinner before the reopening, and what a great night we had, sharing memories of those glory days – of why Geordie Stobart, not Jackie, took the penalty against Fulham in a crucial promotion game, of the Cup semi-final defeat by Charlton in 1947, of the Cup triumphs of the 1950s, and of the new promise after Kevin Keegan had signed as a player. Jackie was, as befits real heroes, a gentleman as well as a great player, and the crowds that turned up for his publicised reopening of the store demonstrated their genuine affection for him. This was over twenty-five years since he had last played at St James'.

From one great hero of the past, the torch of hope had already been passed to the next superhero, who heralded a new dawn in which the latent promise of years might be fulfilled at last. Kevin Keegan, the young player whose 2 goals had put Newcastle United to the sword in the 1974 FA Cup Final – even though United had fielded a Cassidy in their 11 – was the catalyst of the club's revival in the 1980s. He had left Liverpool for Europe, and had twice won the title 'European Player of the Year'. In the process, he had become the first UK footballer millionaire.

His physical appearance was as distinctive as his bustling all-action style of playing, and his transfer to Newcastle in 1982 was so unthinkable it was greeted first with disbelief and then with delirious excitement. At last, somebody was taking the issue of the club's unfulfilled potential seriously. His impact on results and attendances was immediate. In his first season, 1982/83, he played in 41 of the 46 matches and scored 27 goals. The following season, he played in 44 of the 45 matches, scoring 28 goals.

Much more importantly, he led the team to promotion in 1984, restoring it to its rightful position in the ranks of the top clubs of the First Division. He rekindled the hope that United could now enter another golden period. As a result, the average attendance almost doubled in that time, from 17,000 to 30,000, and he retired as a player at the peak of his achievements.

It was not only on the pitch that he made a lasting impression. He brought with him a new desire to invest in sponsorship, particularly from Newcastle Breweries, who benefited directly from his enthusiastic participation in their PR activities in return for their having borne some part of the cost of securing him. His constant exposure to fans created an atmosphere of excited anticipation on match days, as fans arrived earlier than ever for home games. Sales of replica shirts and other memorabilia soared at the club shop, the developing secondary source of income underlining the growing affluence of fans as well as the commercial value of success.

As the prospect of future triumphs was dreamed of, he was gone, in scenes more reminiscent of a Hollywood tearjerker than solid, earthy Tyneside. Wor Kev, as he was now affectionately known, left for retirement as music blared and floodlights played, and to the tears and cheers of the fans he was plucked by helicopter from the centre circle of the playing area he had graced. The supporters loved him, and he reciprocated. The son of a miner from County Durham had come home, albeit briefly, and they had taken him to their hearts.

Arthur Cox, the Manager who had persuaded Keegan to come, and justifiably broke the bank to pay for him, left simultaneously. Stan Seymour, whose father played in the winning 1924 FA Cup side, had been the director who had managed team affairs at Newcastle in post-war soccer and been on the Board for many years, was responsible for the selection of a Manager to replace Cox. He chose Jack Charlton, and Jack, despite being a Geordie, Jackie Milburn's cousin, and a pitman's son, inexplicably lost the plot, abandoning the Cox/Keegan style of all-out attack so beloved by the fans. Predictably, attendances slumped as the team hung around mid-table. Jack Charlton left after a year and in came one of the former goalkeepers, Willie McFaul, to take over. When Beardsley and Waddle left in search of a club that could satisfy their career ambitions, McFaul tried to replace these highly talented players. But his three-year run as Manager ended with relegation in 1989. They finished at the bottom of the First Division with only 31 points, having won more games away than at home. McFaul had a very unhappy, unsuccessful reign. For the first time in the club's history, fans began publicly demonstrating – first against the Board, then the team, then individual players.

Whether this was born out of the sense of loss that followed the departure of Keegan, or the unrest that was infecting football supporters throughout the UK, is difficult to know. But the activist stirrings of some would-be shareholders fanned the flames, intentionally or otherwise. When would the Board learn?

Seriously talented players had arrived at the club. Not only local lads Chris Waddle, who had preceded Keegan, and Peter Beardsley, but later Paul Gascoigne. They all left because they could see neither pleasure nor a future in staying.

Other more successful clubs took advantage of the unrest to 'tap' those players and encourage them to seek a transfer away from the unhealthy atmosphere at this once fiercely loyal and supportive club. Worse still, the not-inconsiderable income from those transfers was squandered on second-rate replacements who failed repeatedly. As familiar failings persisted, the future looked bleak: erratic performances, falling attendance, frequent changes of Manager, and, inevitably, an attempted takeover.

The same old remedies were applied once again with the appointment of another Manager, the experienced Jim Smith. The problems multiplied. Stan Seymour resigned as Chairman and was succeeded by Gordon McKeag. For an inexperienced Chairman, it was to be a baptism of fire.

Gordon McKeag had been a director since the early 1970s and had been involved with the club from boyhood, thanks to his father's Board membership. Having succeeded Stan Seymour as Chairman, it was he who had to lead a board facing demands from all quarters for immediate action to be taken.

From the Government there was already pressure for clubs to take active steps to control hooliganism, to which was added the need for major investment to convert St James' Park into an all-seater stadium. McKeag also faced pressure from his new Manager, who needed adequate funds to rebuild the playing strength, from the Football Association, who made it clear that Newcastle would be excluded from the new Premier League negotiations unless they could quickly gain promotion, and from the fans, who wanted him and his board to resign. With declining attendances in a decaying stadium, the club's debts mounting and the team wallowing in the Second Division, it was a near-impossible task ... or was it?

The most persistent and unpleasant pressure had come from the emergence of a unified attempt to take control of the club. There had been random attempts from individual shareholders in recent years to instigate change by seeking election to the Board, but this time it was different. For the last two years, opposition had formalised around Malcolm Dix, whose family had been shareholders in the club since its earliest days, and who had been joined by the newly formed Newcastle Supporters' Association. What made the group a real threat was its recruitment of John Hall, an increasingly public presence, to their cause. Branding this alliance 'the Magpie Group', they had attracted the support of the main local newspaper, the *Evening Chronicle*, and this was to prove an unstoppable force. By 1988, John Hall had used his wealth to acquire shares. The aggressive prices he offered for the limited number of issued shares proved too attractive to resist, even for some long-time allies of McKeag.

This was followed by the carefully orchestrated launch of a charter for change, styled 'A Pledge for the Future' and subtitled 'Business and Development Strategy'. Heavy emphasis was laid on 'democratising' the club, and the need for substantial investment as a precursor to success. The whole campaign, in style and cost, bore the signature of John Hall, as did the letter to shareholders that introduced it. It also introduced a plan to raise money by an offer of ten million new shares, open to all fans, thus laying a foundation for supporter democracy. Many a man would have given way. McKeag refused to do that, but his health did. He succumbed to serious heart problems, which required major heart surgery.

The decade was to end and the last decade of the old century was to open with a huge question mark hanging over the club's, and its Chairman's, chances of survival.

Things are Bad
and About to Get Worse

When the 1989/90 season ended in the spring, Newcastle missed promotion to the First Division yet again, although only by a narrow margin, having scored 80 goals with the very good squad of players Jim Smith had assembled. Nevertheless, it was a hugely disappointing outcome for Smith, the players, and, most importantly, the long-suffering fans.

The form of the new centre forward star, Micky Quinn, and the attractive attacking football he played, were a hint of better things to come – but that wasn't yet enough for the fans. If the club was to be able to concentrate on playing football, something had to give. Uneasy peace broke out between John Hall and Gordon McKeag, who accepted the inevitability of his hostile adversary joining the Board sooner rather than later. He was already the largest single shareholder – or rather his company, Cameron Hall Developments, was. His campaign for Board membership was irresistible, but the terms of that were being haggled over.

Many local businessmen/football fans believed he was an ideal front man to lead the campaign to wrest control from the families who had effectively owned Newcastle throughout its 100-year history. They included David Stephenson, the Managing Director of Newcastle Breweries Ltd, who had recently allowed his company's shirt sponsorship to lapse. The season ticket holders at St James' were well aware of John Hall's achievements through the growing appeal in the North East of his now-established MetroCentre, and the supporters' own organisation, the NSA, had welcomed the alliance with him, just as they would have welcomed any arrangement that offered a return to success for Newcastle United. Much of this trust in John Hall was built on the simple premise that the miraculous transformation he had achieved on the wasteland outside the city walls he could also achieve within the walls of 'Fortress St James'. The question was, how and by whom would that transformation be achieved?

The answer, for John Hall, was by using his wealth, drive and charisma to break the long-standing family monopoly control of the McKeag, Westwood, and Seymour family dynasties and by replacing it with a 'Democratic, Popular, Fan-owned Club', which had become the slogan of the newly formed 'Magpie Group'.

In the bargaining that ensued, John Hall was offered a seat on the Board and acceptance that his offer of ten million new shares would be adopted when the 1990/91 season kicked off. Thus, the first season of the new decade began with Newcastle United in the Second Division as a new structure for the top division of English football was being negotiated and squabbled over prior to the now-imminent creation of a self-governing 'Premier League' in which Newcastle was not going to figure until they were reinstated in the First Division.

Pressure for change in the long-standing structure of the football leagues had been evidenced years earlier through a threat by ten clubs to form a breakaway league, severing all links with the FA and the Football League. It had resulted in repeated attempts to negotiate a solution acceptable to both parties that would not damage the attractiveness and prospects for football nationally. The catalyst for change was of course money: that of satellite TV broadcasters seeking to break the BBC monopoly.

Perhaps in the war raging over control of Newcastle United this crucial issue had been relegated in importance, because John Hall and his supporters were deflecting the attention of Gordon McKeag, the current Newcastle Chairman but importantly also a member of the FA Management Committee. Did the threat of exclusion from the Premiership take a backseat to the immediacy of local issues? Perhaps no one had yet grasped the financial significance and other consequences of the change? Whatever the reasons, there was to be a heavy price to pay as a result of this failure.

In April, John Hall joined the Board, which had already been reshaped a year earlier by three new directors: Peter Mallinger and Bob Young, both with substantial shareholdings in the club, and a promoted executive, Russell Cushing. A prospectus for an offer of eight million new shares at £1 per 50p share – aimed at fans but open to the public – was issued on 29 October 1990 with a closing date of 30 November if the minimum subscription for new shares fell short of £2.5 million, although if that minimum figure was achieved it could remain open until 31 January 1991. John Hall, holding over three million shares, was by far the largest single shareholder and held an overall majority.

The speculation was immense, and it seemed inevitable that both John and his new democracy would triumph. It failed spectacularly. With less than half the minimum sum subscribed, which represented less than a fifth of the hoped-for subscription, the grand scheme of the Magpie Group lay in tatters.

The Board was in disarray; an expensive misjudgement had been made. The club was perilously short of new money, and the team, after the promise of the previous season's strong finish, was now in 16th place.

Something had to give and Gordon McKeag, accepting full responsibility, stood down from the Chair. At first, it seemed to be the opening John Hall was seeking, but he was not invited to chair the Board; George Forbes succeeded. Chastened by the failure of the fund-raising attempt, Hall resigned, taking a nominal role as Vice President.

However, his son Douglas was appointed to the Board, notionally as a representative of the Magpie Group. The 1990/91 season followed a now-familiar pattern – early promise, followed by defeats, a failure to gain promotion, a narrow avoidance of relegation to the Third Division, declining attendances, rising debt, and, as a result, a managerial sacking before the season ended. However, a new Manager with fan appeal and a track record as an international footballer, the Argentinian Ossie Ardiles, was appointed to replace Jim Smith as the team ended the season in 11th place. A new season, a new Manager … surely things would improve?

Not in the Boardroom. Surprisingly, Douglas Hall quit in May, leaving the Hall family, the largest shareholder, outside the walls of St James' at a crucial time. Further disruption was inevitable.

Performance on the pitch didn't improve either, even though Ardiles introduced a blend of local talent and some shrewdly purchased younger players. In lowering the age of the squad, he was preparing for a longer term than he was to be allowed. In the meantime, he encouraged his young team to play in a style that won the hearts and minds of Geordies. Essentially, though, his young team lacked the experience to grind out results and their league position deteriorated rapidly. By November, they had slumped to the bottom of the Second Division as open warfare broke out yet again for control of the club, leading this time to John Hall's appointment as Chairman and a 'night of long knives'. Out went Gordon McKeag and Stan Seymour – who was also the club's President. The shape of things to come was Douglas Hall and two new faces, David McVickers and Freddy Shepherd, the new Vice Chairman, who arrived to 'strengthen the Board'.

The fans were delighted. Here was the local lad, with money to support his frequently articulated, colourfully exaggerated ambitions. Hall was surely one whose business knowledge would at last get United out of its self-destructive rut of mismanagement and unplanned, profligate spending on second-rate players. If he could achieve half of what he had achieved with MetroCentre, the future looked brighter than it had for twenty years.

Totally in character, he made some interesting and well-publicised early comments, such as, 'I never wanted this job.' And then the standard, doom-laden, 'Ossie has my full support and is the best man for the job.'

Determined to refashion the club's internal operations and optimise its income from sources other than ticket sales, he also engaged, initially on a consultancy basis, the Commercial Director of Glasgow Rangers, Freddie Fletcher, a former Liberal politician with an impressive record at the Scottish club.

Unfortunately, far from improving, the team's performance continued to be erratic and their league position was in free fall after a series of bad results culminating in defeats, first in the FA Cup at St James' to lowly Bournemouth, and then to Oxford United 2-5 in February 1992. There was deep concern, but one voice above all – that of Freddie Fletcher – argued not only that an immediate change of Manager was essential, but that the replacement had to be Kevin Keegan. After a few days of frenetic activity that would have done justice to any thriller script, Ardiles had gone, with the Chairman's 'deep regret', and Keegan was installed with the usual self-congratulatory welcome and the Chairman's guarantee that 'this time things really are going to be different'.

Tyneside was delirious again, but not for long. Amid the clamour, relationships on the Board ruptured yet again. Despite the rise in attendances after Keegan's second coming, debts were unsustainable and mounting, just as the Chairman was faced with the new Manager's expensive wish list. The Board could not agree on or obtain the bank facilities needed, and with the club sliding towards the Third Division, Kevin did what he was to repeat in future and walked out a mere forty days after he had agreed to return.

Sir John now knew that he alone could break the deadlock and, at the price of assuming full control and virtually absolute ownership with a handful of shareholding supporters, he bankrolled the club using personal guarantees. Nothing short of this would entice Keegan to return or prevent his investment, his reputation, and his pride from going with Newcastle United 'down the drain'.

There were new signings and some improvement in results, but Newcastle still travelled to Leicester on the closing day of the season believing that to lose would not only result in relegation but the end of the dream, perhaps forever. While a draw might just be enough, their survival would be dependent on the other struggler's results. A win was needed desperately.

At the time, I was unaware of the drama that had preceded Kevin Keegan's third (or was it fourth?) coming, but like every fan, I was less concerned with high jinks and politics and more with the pressing issue of what I could do to rescue my beloved Newcastle United from its desperate plight, and the unthinkable consequences if we lost. The solution, of course, was to be there with someone who had lived through more than one of these cliffhanging episodes previously. Who better than my younger brother, Sydney? He had, after all, been with me when we had willed

Newcastle to overcome Sheffield Wednesday in an equally important match that clinched their 1948 bid for promotion.

On the bright sunny morning of 2 May 1992, we set off for Filbert Street, Leicester, for the crucial game, but not before putting a bottle of champagne in the fridge, on Napoleon's rationale that 'in victory you deserve it and in defeat you need it'. I was suitably dressed with a 'Blue Star' crested Newcastle shirt beneath my formal shirt, tie, and jacket. As we parked, I remembered that it was 2,000 Guineas Day at Newmarket and that I had intended to place a small bet on Lester Piggott's mount Rodrigo de Triano to win, which I immediately corrected with a phone call from the car. But hurdles still remained. A cordon of police near the ground was turning away Toon supporters in their droves and Sydney queried the reason as we passed scrutiny. We were told that it was because they were 'wearing Newcastle United shirts which might be provocative to home supporters'. My brother helpfully pointed out that I, too, was wearing a Newcastle shirt, but the policeman smilingly confirmed that I passed muster because it was covered. There's nothing like brotherly love to remind one of how hard life's struggles can be.

At last, we were in, and before we took our seats I demonstrated my total commitment to the cause by placing a further wager predicting that Newcastle would win 2-1 and that Peacock would score the first goal. In a scrappy, untidy game, so it turned out. He did and they did and when I switched on the car radio, so had Lester Piggott. Seldom had victory, or the vintage champagne we consumed on our return, tasted sweeter. Why? The reality remained that Newcastle were anchored at the bottom of the Second Division. Keegan's record was not one of permanency, and pledges of support had yet to be transformed into progress.

The Board had still to cope with the shortage of funds and it was now certain they would miss out on the first Premiership season. However, it was a step in the right direction, and if they could finish in the top three in the 1992/93 season, they could be back in the Premiership before it was too late. For all football fans most of the time, but for Geordies always, optimism needs very little encouragement to flourish – was it to be justified this time?

Before the month had ended, Sir John's company Cameron Hall Developments Ltd had made an unconditional offer for the shares which they did not already own. When the offer closed on 6 July 1992, CHD held 87.64% of the issued shares. A formal statement read, 'Newcastle United is now a subsidiary undertaking of Cameron Hall Developments Ltd.'

The Board of Newcastle United was reformed to reflect its new status. On 7 July, out went Forbes, Mallinger, McVickers, and Young, and in came a CHD director, Russell Jones, who joined the two Halls, Sir John and Douglas, and Freddy Shepherd. It was 100 years, almost to the day, since Newcastle United had been born. What lay ahead?

5

Hall of Fame

John Hall was now unstoppable and the Boardroom reflected his primacy. Newcastle United substituted one group of controlling families for another, this time the Halls and the Shepherds. More accurately, perhaps, it was run and funded by the family businesses of these two clans, and in consequence, by some of their key executives.

The top directors were listed as Sir John Hall – Chairman, and Freddy Shepherd – Deputy Chairman; the other directors were Douglas Hall, Sir John's son, and Russell Jones, the Managing Director of Cameron Hall. Freddy Shepherd and his brother Bruce owned Shepherd Offshore. The other three directors were the Board of Cameron Hall Developments, Sir John's principal company. Freddie Fletcher had the title of Chief Executive. He was the only one with any experience of club management, but he didn't have a seat on the Board.

That it might lack some balance of experience and perspective was unlikely to be questioned by the fans. Sir John had brought hope and promise and had demonstrated already the financial 'clout' he could use to fund his publicly declared ambitions. However, if these were to be anything but fantasy, the first objective was to escape the newly designated First Division with its strange-looking assortment of clubs.

Newcastle made a cracking start, fuelling the wildest dreams, as they reeled off 12 league wins on the trot – admittedly against the likes of Southend, Bristol Rovers, Bristol City, Brentford, and Tranmere – before they lost, against Grimsby of all teams, at home on 24 October. The jitters started when they lost the next week at Leicester followed by a no-score draw at home to Swindon, but they pulled themselves together again with another promising sequence of 4 consecutive wins.

Concerns were increasing, not only because of the erratic results, but also because of the quality of the opposition when compared to that which they would face in the Premiership. The worries mounted rapidly as they dropped points in December. They recovered briefly, but in January and February the team could only manage 6 draws and 2 defeats in the six weeks between beating Peterborough 3-0 on 16 January – Robert Lee's debut – and a 3-0 victory over Tranmere on 28 February.

There was only one solution, and it was Keegan's intuitive grasp and inbred instinct, backed by Hall's money, that would solve it. Simply, another top-quality striker was needed. Kelly's goals had dried up in this bad patch – he had scored only once in 9 games – and there was still a long road ahead.

This period taught Keegan a lot, not only about assembling a squad which could seriously challenge for honours, but also about the difficulties of his relationship with the Board. Shepherd and both Halls were involved in every aspect of the club's management. For the moment, however, the relationship was working. Keegan and his scouts produced what was needed and by mid-March a new striking star, Andy Cole, was ready for action. He had cost £1.75 million within a total spend of £3 million on three new players. Newcastle finished the season in a blaze of glory, demolishing Leicester 7-1 at home on the last day of the season, in front of the customary sea of black and white shirts and, most importantly, with a huge TV audience thrilled by the action. Keegan's eye for, and ability to attract, quality players was evident and the fans loved him for it.

They had done it and fast-tracked into the Premiership. Incredibly, it was only a year since its opening, when Newcastle had been at the bottom of the pack contesting promotion places. But their first Premiership season proved to be a tough baptism, with only 1 point from the first 3 games, in a game away to Manchester United. After 8 games, the team were below mid-table, with Chelsea behind them and Liverpool ahead, but as they continued to acclimatise, they grew in confidence and climbed up the league table. They were 4th after 18 games and finished the season in 3rd place behind Manchester United and Blackburn Rovers. The Board had set the playing staff's incentive bonus target as achieving 8th place, so everyone was delighted with the final placing.

Peter Beardsley had returned and Cole had proved a prolific goal scorer. Creditable though it was, and happy though the fans were, Keegan knew he had to strengthen his squad further. The combination of his appeal to aspiring players, Newcastle's attractive, entertaining style, and Sir John's readiness to back his inspirational Manager's choices with cash, permitted an inflow of top-quality continental players, which began with the signings of Albert from Belgium and Hottiger from Switzerland.

Both demonstrated another basic tenet of Keegan's approach to the challenge of the Premiership: all his 11 players should be genuine footballers, comfortable on the ball and capable of playing in a fluid formation to provide maximum support for two or three out-and-out strikers.

He demanded that the emphasis be on scoring goals and playing fast, passing football. Footballing defenders, not stoppers, were a prerequisite.

Yet, after a promising start in the 1994/95 season, and despite playing attractive attacking football, they could only finish 6th, and the first signs of tension began to appear in the Newcastle camp. Keegan knew intuitively where he needed to strengthen his squad, but the target was moving away from him as every Premiership club responded to the increased competition arising from the league's international appeal and increasing TV income. The financial pressures on the club were growing daily.

Increased transfer fees and rapidly escalating salaries couldn't be met without further income. Freddie Fletcher had improved sponsorship, merchandise sales, and corporate hospitality income, but the ground capacity was still only 36,000 and demand exceeded this by a wide margin. There had been some ground improvements and there were ongoing planning discussions with the City Council, but the inescapable fact was that money was tight. In moves that surprised many and shocked others, Newcastle sold Andy Cole for £7 million and bought Gillespie, Ferdinand, and Ginola. Whatever anyone thought, it proved to be an inspired move. Early in the 1995/96 season, the new players powered Newcastle to the top of the Premiership, hotly pursued by Manchester United.

By the end of October, they were the only Premiership team with a 100 per cent home record and had only dropped 4 points away from St James', giving them a 2-point lead over the reigning Champions, Manchester United. They had earned one of those points away to Manchester early in the season, and by the time the two met at St James' early in March 1996, they had doubled that advantage to 4 points with only 11 games to play, including 'one in hand' over their rivals, a potential lead of 7 points that would rise to a massive lead of 10 points – if they won the match.

It was a Monday evening match and the city was in a state of feverish excitement as I arrived by train from London, to which I had to return on the 7.00 a.m. train the next morning. I could feel the tension in the air on my short walk from the County Hotel, opposite the Central Station, as I heard the excited chatter of fans in the packed pubs I passed on my way to the ground. They were downing their pre-match beer and gloating over the probability of an unassailable lead for Newcastle after the keenly anticipated victory.

The same quickened pulse was evident in the private box to which I had been invited by my Geordie hosts, although it was balanced by the presence of other guests from Manchester. In an atmosphere of nervous anticipation, the first half was played in a cauldron of ear-splitting noise the like of which you seldom hear. While Newcastle dominated possession with virtually every shot on goal, Schmeichel, the Manchester goalkeeper, had one of his purple patches. He was almost single-handedly responsible for Manchester's clean sheet at the interval. 'We gave them a nil-nil thrashing in the first half,' Keegan said to TV commentators at half-time, and he was right. The second half started with the same one-way traffic as the first, but as the minutes ticked by I had the awful sensation that every fan has experienced – that today is just not your day! So it proved to be. Cantona, with an incisive strike, drilled home the winning goal from close range, with one of the handful of opportunities that Manchester had created. 'C'est la vie,' Ginola and Albert probably muttered, with Gallic shrugs. 'Bugger,' said I, with feeling. The bubble of optimism that had preceded the game had been punctured not just in the box but throughout the deserted city centre, in the empty pubs, and on the quiet streets as I returned to the hotel.

Knowing I had a 10.30 a.m. meeting with some Japanese executives, which would continue all day and over dinner that night, I breakfasted on the 7.00 a.m. train, read the papers, and reflected on the game. I concluded that while it was a disappointing setback, it was far from a terminal blow. After all, we were still top, we still had a game in hand, and we had now played Manchester twice. Liverpool, in 3rd place, were a further 5 points adrift of them. Cool heads were needed at St James' to send an encouraging message to the players. True, after 14 successive home wins, the Premiership's only 100 per cent record had gone. But with an attack that included Asprilla, Beardsley, Ferdinand, Ginola, and Lee and had scored 52 goals already, Newcastle were still favourites for the title. My reasoning was not purely the returning optimism of the football fan; it was the logic of a seasoned businessman who had been through similar situations many times before.

As I walked back through the carriages to my reserved seat, I came across John Hall, who had joined the train at Darlington and was having a snack in his seat. I knew him very well now, having met him many times in London and Newcastle since our initial meeting on the MetroCentre site over ten years earlier. I remember the conversation vividly.

'Pity about last night, John. And I really think we were very unlucky to lose all 3 points.'

'It's a disaster,' replied John, unsmilingly.

'No, it's not! We only play them twice, and they are out of the way now. We are still a point in front, which we should be able to convert to four. Come on, John. We've lost a battle, not the war.'

'It's a complete disaster, a total disaster. We've blown it and I told Kevin so last night.'

'You didn't?'

'I did and it is.'

I left him brooding and returned to my seat, knowing that a time bomb was ticking. I hoped, but no longer believed, that this thrilling side would crown a wonderfully entertaining season by winning the Premiership title.

By the time the season entered its last week, Newcastle were 6 points behind Manchester United, but still with a game in hand when they played Leeds in another night game on 29 April. They won, despite the pressure, but fatally failed to beat Nottingham Forest three nights later. They went into the last game of the season knowing that only if they won and Manchester United lost they would be Champions.

An extract from Kevin Keegan's programme notes before that match reflected what I had suspected for the last two months. He was a man in turmoil over his perceived failure. 'Everybody connected with this club – every fan and every neutral up and down the country will have their own interpretation as to why one club won or lost it. My own feelings are that I'll be desperately disappointed if we're runners-up, because I believed from day one we could be Champions.'

The following page carried, unusually, a message from the Chairman, headed, 'Chairman Sir John Hall says'. It read, 'This is just the beginning. The best is yet to come.' It was accompanied by a photograph of Sir John in a replica strip.

But the key message, at least for me, was this: 'We've always known that the psychological barrier we have to break is to win something.'

The pressure wasn't coming only from Alex Ferguson, it was also coming from within the club, and the real struggle now was in Kevin Keegan's own mind.

Newcastle faltered to a draw, Manchester United beat Middlesbrough to become Champions again, and Newcastle finished as runners-up. Disappointing? Yes, but after such a marvellously exciting season, most fans were already looking forward to August and more excitement, even if it was going to be in the rollercoaster way that typified the club's style. In addition they would play in Europe again, even if it was not yet in the Champions League, to put the seal of ultimate success on a club so close to restoring its position at the very pinnacle of English football.

The question was: what was going to happen in the close season, before the 1996/97 Premiership kicked off, to improve Newcastle United's prospects?

6

The End of a Glorious Dream

Most football fans were preoccupied in the close season with England hosting Euro '96 rather than their own team's affairs, a happy distraction for Newcastle fans still brooding over last season's 'almost but not quite' title bid. It was probably much the same for most football mangers, too. For the wealthiest and most successful Premiership clubs, the competition offered a shop window full of talented players – the best in Europe all playing competitively on their own doorstep. England reached the semi-finals before losing to Germany on penalties, although Alan Shearer scored his penalty in that game and became the top scorer of the tournament.

Perhaps this set off a chain reaction in Alex Ferguson's mind. Newcastle had given him a fright in the domestic season that had just ended. Blackburn, Shearer's club, had won the title the previous season and Manchester had scored fewer goals in 1995/96 than they had in either of the 2 preceding seasons. The news broke that Ferguson was close to finalising the signing of the Premiership's leading goal scorer for an undisclosed fee should have been anticipated, but it wasn't. Newcastle moved swiftly to stake their claim, and paid a world record fee of £15 million to bring Shearer to St James' Park. Why was this unsurprising? Simply because Shearer was born a Geordie. He had followed the club as a boy and had a great admiration for Keegan, a boyhood hero. He was also, of course, coming home as a hero, even though he would have the weight of great expectations to carry, not least those of John Hall.

John Hall was desperate for success now. His publicly stated ambitions became ever more expansive. All that was needed was for him to foot the bill – not only the huge transfer fee, but also an eye-watering salary. He had sold MetroCentre the previous year, banking a large profit, but was committed to another large property development at Wynyard Hall, on the estate he had acquired with his grand country home. He had personally guaranteed the club's debts, but that couldn't go on forever, even though the rising income streams were reassuring.

There was a new stadium to be funded; a maximum capacity of 36,500 was sub-optimising the income opportunity, even if it was packed every week.

It was then that his thoughts hardened into outline plans for an early London Stock Exchange listing, a step that should only have provided the finance needed to satisfy his ambitions but which, with hindsight, was the beginning of the end of the dream.

But back to the pitch. After all the pre-season euphoria, the press conferences and parading, reality dawned with the first game of the season. Newcastle lost 0-2 at Everton, despite an attack including Shearer, Ferdinand, Ginola, and Gillespie, supported by Lee. Beardsley was on the bench. A win four days later against Wimbledon was followed by another defeat away to Sheffield Wednesday. As August ended, Newcastle was 14th in the league.

This was not what was expected. Pressure mounted, to which the team responded magnificently, with 6 successive wins. After 9 matches, they were top of the table. Keegan, the fans, the team, and Sir John intended to stay there, but to do so they must first lay the ghost of the previous year's home defeat by Manchester United. However, Manchester United were unbeaten in the season so far, and they were to be the visitors in the next match at St James' on Sunday 20 October. Before that, there was a lengthy midweek trip to Hungary to face Ferencváros in a televised UEFA Cup second round tie, which Newcastle lost in a five-goal thriller. It was enough to have nerves jangling in Newcastle before the 4.00 p.m. kick-off against their title rivals.

Keegan's pre-match programme notes revealed the extent of the scars he carried following the 0-1 home defeat only seven months previously: '… Peter Schmeichel and Eric Cantona. Their standards were magnificent … when we played well enough in the first half to have sunk Manchester Utd without trace … Cantona grabbing the goal that separated the teams and cut our lead to a single point.'

Those nightmarish memories had only been reinforced by Manchester United's demolition of Newcastle 0-4 in the pre-season Charity Shield match at Wembley. Both Philippe Albert and the club captain, Peter Beardsley, now restored as a first choice, contributed similar remorse-filled comments to the programme notes. Dwelling on the same 2 games did not bode well for Toon supporters, as evidenced by the nervous anticipation of this match.

There were plenty of reminders that Newcastle had never beaten Manchester United in a Premier League match, home or away. But defeat them they did: 5-0 on that Sunday afternoon, in an exhilarating display of football by the whole team. The two central defenders, Peacock and Albert, opened and closed the scoring, with three attackers, Shearer, Ferdinand, and Ginola, each adding a goal between. The final whistle came with Newcastle still attacking and the crowd baying for six while the public address system announced to roars of approval, 'The Man of the Match award goes to every player in the Newcastle side.'

Surely now, with a 3-point advantage and only 10 games played, they would win the league? Keegan's post-match comments in *The Times* were very different to the stressed, apprehensive tone of the pre-match programme. Now he was quoted as saying, 'I awoke yesterday to criticism, some of it from top people, about the way we are doing it. We opened up today, we played *our* way, we proved that the League can be won by attacking football, as we should have done last season.'

The city was convinced, souvenirs were made, a special supplement was produced by the local paper, and Keegan mania held the population in thrall. In truth, it was vintage Keegan, and the team's display had touched the heights … from which they quickly fell.

Sadly, Shearer, who was injured, missed the next 7 games after having scored in each of the last 4 games. Although his absence was a big blow, the squad was awash with talent – Asprilla, Clark, and Gillespie had been on the bench for the Manchester match. Yet Newcastle lost the next game away to Leicester without scoring, and immediately slipped to 2nd place.

The team regained top spot with a 3-1 victory at home to Middlesbrough, and retained it following 2 successive draws against London clubs. Shearer returned, fully recovered, and scored on each of his two appearances as the season neared the halfway mark. On the last day of November, Arsenal, in 2nd place and only a single point behind Newcastle, were the visitors to St James'. Manchester United, having never recovered from the defeat at St James', appeared to be out of the race and languished in 7th place, 6 points adrift. Although Ferdinand was now injured and absent and Asprilla was deputising, hopes of a victory to consolidate their lead at the top were high.

Shearer dutifully scored a goal, but it was Newcastle's only goal against Arsenal's two as the Gunners leapfrogged Newcastle, to lead by 2 points. Newcastle then dropped to 3rd place, and by Boxing Day this had deteriorated to 6th, with only 2 points gained from 4 league matches in December.

During this catastrophic month, the Newcastle Board confirmed what many knew privately with the announcement on 19 December that they intended to seek a listing on the London Stock Exchange, on a date yet to be agreed early in 1997. Three new appointments had been made. The Board would be joined by the two Joint Chief Executives and a Finance Director. There are more appropriate times to announce a fundraising plan.

One thing was clear: this was not going to be a closed issue to local supporters. Remember there had been a promise to 'democratise' the ownership and management of the club 'by the people, for the people', which John Hall had sponsored in the failed fundraising scheme of 1990, and for the failure of which his predecessor, Gordon McKeag, had forfeited his job and shares. But now that he, his son, and Freddy Shepherd were the principal owners, it was going to be a public offering, attracting institutional support which would clear the club's debts, redeem the Cameron Hall guarantees, and provide the club with a 'war chest' for further investment. It would also, of course, make a healthy 'book profit' for the Hall and Shepherd families, who would continue to hold a significant majority of the shares after the flotation.

The only problem now was that the plan, signed off in the euphoric mood of the October victory over Manchester United, might look less attractive in the present climate. The pressure exerted on Kevin Keegan was enormous and it showed in every post-match interview, whether he was speaking in defeat or victory. In private, his volatile mood caused sufficient concern for his salary to be increased and a longer-term contract to be agreed, but still the tensions increased.

As the year drew to a close, Newcastle signed off in true Keegan style with a crushing 7-1 defeat of Spurs in which Lee, Ferdinand, and Shearer each scored 2 goals and Albert completed the scoring. They then opened the New Year with a convincing 3-0 victory over Leeds on 1 January and 2 successive, much-needed home wins, which pushed them up to 4th place.

As is, was, and always will be on Tyneside, hope came flooding back. The past month had been a blip, that's all. Regrettable, yes, but with 15 games still to play the mood was, 'King Kev can do it – howay the lads!'

I left the UK for a holiday in Australia the day after Spurs were put to the sword and, as has been my habit for most of my life, I eagerly caught up with the details of the win over Leeds, this time on Australian TV. The weather was glorious, the beach on which we had rented a house was delightful, and, given the 2 victories on Tyneside, I was in a very relaxed frame of mind.

Nothing had prepared me for the shock I had as I woke and prepared for an early morning swim after a cup of tea one day. I was catching up with world news on ABC Radio, when an Australian announcer, speaking in a grave tone, said they were going over 'to our reporter in the UK for news of a shock resignation'. Interesting, I thought – John Major, perhaps?

Then another Australian voice took up the tale: 'A story of a resignation that has shaken the football world to its foundations has just been announced. Kevin Keegan has resigned as Manager of Newcastle United, but that's all we know, so I am ringing the club's line to see if I can get further news.'

In a state of disbelief, I listened to the phone ringing 13,000 miles away and then the pre-recorded message, in a female Geordie voice, saying, 'Yes! It's true; Kevin Keegan has resigned as Manager of Newcastle United today. The club has nothing more to say at this stage but will be making a further statement later.' Then I heard the dialling tone again. I sat down to digest the news. How had this happened? Why had it happened? What really lay behind this news? Whatever answers emerged, it was now world news, and no longer a local Tyneside drama.

One thing was certain; the dream was over, gone ... The beautiful game at its best – played with freedom and style, attacking and entertaining – was, for the moment at least, just a memory.

The season wasn't over, but who could pick Newcastle up now and infuse them with belief now that Kevin Keegan was gone and with him the joy and pride he had brought to the club and its fans?

Life must go on, and by the time I returned to London on 21 January, Keegan had been replaced by another Liverpool old boy, Kenny Dalglish. Undeniably, the new manager was a talented goal-scoring footballer who had recent experience successfully managing a Premier League club, but his taciturn demeanour was a marked contrast to Keegan's infectious *joie de vivre*. What I learned subsequently was that strenuous efforts had been made to persuade Barcelona to release Bobby Robson, which they had flatly refused to do, and to get Bobby to walk out, which he rejected with equal firmness, even though he was desperately keen to return to Tyneside, on the grounds he 'had never broken a contract' in his life. I personally believed at the time that the haste of the decision to sign Dalglish was driven more to protect the stock market listing process than it was a considered choice of the best person to carry on Keegan's work. That led me to ask again the question of why Keegan had walked away, and the answer to that lay in how well anyone in the club really understood Keegan and his strategy.

Soon, my lifelong interest in football, and Newcastle United in particular, took a strange, wonderful, and entirely unexpected twist. I was invited to meet the Board of Newcastle United to explore our mutual interest in my becoming a non-executive director, which would enable the club to satisfy one of the requirements of the Stock Exchange Listing Rules.

The date agreed was Sunday 2 February, my birthday and a match day, with a home game against Leicester kicking off after our meeting.

In the course of that meeting, I met Freddy Shepherd and Freddie Fletcher. Douglas Hall and Mark Corbidge, Freddie Fletcher's Joint Chief Executive, were unable to attend. It was a good meeting and I was able to understand the structure, income streams, and stated aims of the Board. It was very clear that Freddie Fletcher was the commercial driver of the club, with a deep knowledge and love of football, learned in childhood and honed commercially at Glasgow Rangers. I said I would be happy to continue discussions with the Board and left them to consider my fitness for the role.

Newcastle won that afternoon and the Board invited me to join them a week later. A different challenge lay before me and the club; it also offered me the opportunity to have some of my own questions answered. Perhaps this was going to provide a way for me to repay the club for the years of enjoyment I had experienced as a fan? My long experience as a company director in other businesses, many of them family-owned or family-dominated, meant that I was under no misapprehension – this was not going to be a sinecure – and I would have to work hard to gain the trust of the Board as a precursor to making any contribution. It would be a very different way of life for the whole Board after the stock exchange listing. I would, for the first time, be a party to the decision-making. Some birthday present!

There was still a season to finish which, after the high promise of October, was set to end in tears. Kenny Dalglish had received a muted welcome and his suitability to walk in Keegan's shoes was being questioned after 2 league draws and an FA Cup defeat at home at the hands of struggling Nottingham Forest. Newcastle had beaten Leicester 4-3 – less than convincingly – on 2 February, retaining their 4th place, as they did for most of the remaining games. A grandstand finish in the last four days of the season, winning a point at Old Trafford and blitzing Nottingham Forest 5-0 at home, made them runners-up to Manchester United yet again, this time 7 points adrift.

Was it really only seven months ago that those margins could have been reversed? Yet there was a consolation prize. In the next season, 1997/98, Newcastle would be competing in the Champions League against the giants of European football for the first time. Hope was being rekindled and doubts about Dalglish were receding, but the remorse over what might have been was still dominant.

The public issue of shares had been announced at the end of February and some fans were now shareholders as well as season ticket holders, which nursed further hope that the inflow of funds from the stock exchange listing would provide ample funds to fulfil the promise of the Keegan years.

If only, if only, if only ...

7

'Bubble, Bubble, Toil and Trouble'

If the 1996/97 season had finished with a late flourish, bringing the runners-up prize of a place in the Champions League, it had still left a widespread feeling of regret that it had been achieved with the squad assembled by Kevin Keegan; there remained the lingering question of why the John Hall/Kevin Keegan partnership had ruptured after five years of publicly affirmed mutual admiration and self-congratulation. To the fans, this mutually supportive relationship was entirely understandable, given the excitement and entertainment they had enjoyed during that period. More than a year earlier in my conversation with John Hall on the London-bound train, I felt I had seen a different face of that relationship, and I felt Keegan's departure was sad and probably avoidable. It was nevertheless a fact, and the most important thing now was to see how Kenny Dalglish intended to build on the platform his predecessor had bequeathed. That would soon be evidenced by whatever changes he made in the playing squad, and by his chosen formations and selections.

There was another significant change required by the stock exchange listing, the effects of which would have an impact in the Boardroom, but were of little interest and not obvious to fans. The preconditions included that Sir John should stand down as Chairman of the PLC and that the Hall family must commit not to exert undue pressure on the PLC Board's processes and decision-making. I knew from long personal experience how difficult the observance of these conditions could be for former owners who were now majority shareholders instead. One of the other conditions was to appoint a number of external directors as non-executives to oversee the Board's activities and ensure that in supporting the executives they protected the rights of minority shareholders. It was this that gave me the opportunity to join the Board and to see from within how the club was really run. I was to be one of three new appointments. The others, whom I would meet later, were the new Chairman, Sir Terence Harrison, a local man with considerable business experience as a company chairman, most recently at Sir Alfred McAlpine, and John Mayo, a former investment banker and now Finance Director of Marconi, formerly the General Electric Company. Unusually, in this case the majority shareholders were both now non-executive directors and remained on the PLC Board, while simultaneously holding key executive positions on the Football Club Board. Freddie Fletcher now held the position Chief Executive on both.

All of this was public knowledge, but was of minimal interest. Yet it was to play the major role in the club's descent into another long period of frustration and decline, as you will see later.

The close season dealings by Dalglish were worrying. Ferdinand, Ginola, Clark, Elliot, and Kitson left – to be replaced by Pistone, Tomasson, Ketsbaia, Hamilton, and Stuart Pearce. Before the season was very old, the veteran Pearce had been joined by two of Dalglish's old Liverpool colleagues, John Barnes and Ian Rush, both in the twilight years of their careers.

It signalled a clear move away from the Keegan plan of having 11 ball-playing, attack-minded individuals, to a formation centred on a cautious defensive midfield. It would eliminate much of the Keegan risk factor, but it was at the expense of the entertainment of audiences, home, away, and on TV. The squad seemed, to me at least, to be incapable of scoring the number of goals required to sustain a challenge for honours and my doubts increased when Newcastle, in pursuit of this plan, agreed a fee for Ferdinand to move to Tottenham. Since I had by then settled in on the Board and had developed a good working relationship with Freddie Fletcher, I asked him to give me the reasons why. He cited Ferdinand's age, his susceptibility to injury, the £6 million fee being offered by Spurs, and the recruitment of the younger, though inexperienced, Jon Dahl Tomasson, of whom Dalglish thought highly, as Shearer's new strike partner.

I asked Freddie one simple question: 'What will we do if Shearer breaks his leg in a pre-season game?'

'Why should he?' answered Freddie.

'Only because that is Sod's Law,' I countered, 'and I have been around long enough to know that the most unlikely things happen at the worst possible time. Don't sell him until we have a proven goal-scorer to replace Les Ferdinand.'

'It's too late anyway,' said Freddie.

The next Saturday evening, I had a phone call from an agitated Freddie, asking angrily, 'How did you know Shearer was going to break his leg today at Goodison Park?'

It had happened, and in the season that followed, neither Newcastle nor Dalglish ever recovered from the loss of their lone star striker, who didn't return to action until the following January.

Despite this devastating blow, they started well enough with 3 consecutive home victories, one in a Champions League qualifier, but when the second leg of the Champions League match away was postponed as well as the Premiership game away at Liverpool – because of Princess Diana's funeral – Newcastle were in 8th place, with the maximum 6 points, and 2 games in hand. Since every team above them had dropped at least 1 point and Newcastle were due to entertain Wimbledon, then the bottom club and without a win, they would surely move further up the table, as and when they played their 2 games in hand. Better still, Barcelona, the European gold standard John Hall had frequently quoted as the model for his Newcastle United, would be their opponents four days later.

A closer look at Dalglish's team selection for the Wimbledon match and the outflow of talent offered a very different prospect. Tomasson's first game in the season's opener had been a disastrous match for him. He had missed an open goal in the first minute and two more later.

Beardsley remained on the bench throughout, and left the club shortly afterwards. Asprilla, who also started as a substitute, came on for Gillespie, and the attacking role was filled by John Barnes and Ian Rush making their Newcastle debuts. The 1-3 defeat by Wimbledon was a self-fulfilling prophecy and the hitherto unbeaten team was now in 12th place, after a performance that deserved no better.

Disappointing performances are soon erased from fans' memories, though, and excited anticipation was almost as high in the city on Wednesday 17 September as it had been in March the previous year, although memories of that morale-sapping defeat to Manchester United tempered expectations this time. Nevertheless, the fevered atmosphere, so easy to feel on my favoured walk through the streets of the old town on my way to the ground, was unmistakeable – wagers, hopes, and prayers pleaded for a famous victory to kick-start a new episode and banish those still lingering regrets that King Kev had abdicated.

When the Barcelona players emerged from the tunnel to start the game that night, it may not have looked anything like Nou Camp, but the noise levels of the 35,724 full house would certainly have sounded like it. This time, they delivered; or rather Faustino Asprilla did, with a mesmerising hat trick to defeat the Spanish Champions 3-2 in a famous victory. It took a long time for the stadium to clear that night, but when it did its bedraggled air and the detritus left by a vast crowd were an omen for the season ahead. My foreboding was in marked contrast to the exultant mood of the fans, who were now adding the possibility of a Champions League trophy to their wish list!

The celebratory post-match atmosphere in the Boardroom guest suite that night also suggested something greater had happened. Sir John might no longer be Chairman of the club or the PLC Board but he still 'owned' it, and his rhetoric was in full flow. The victory was 'the benchmark' he had set and proclaimed publicly for years. He would create a 'Barcelona upon Tyne'. Newcastle United was one of the greatest clubs in Europe, and tonight the players had proved it. They would march on to more triumphs, they would continue where Keegan had left off, there would be no shortage of funds to develop the stadium and to buy new players, and ...

Hall continued, to the delight of radio and television reporters. John was ecstatic, and rightly so, but his extrapolation of what had happened was not matched by reality, and nor did he mention what was once his central aim – to democratise the club – for which Barcelona was of course the ideal model.

Newcastle went on to win three out of the next 4 Premiership matches before the slide down the league started again. They also lost the return match at Nou Camp in Barcelona, as well as both matches against PSV Eindhoven, one of Bobby Robson's former clubs, and exited the Champions League without reaching the knock-out stage.

There was only one more realistic opportunity left to satisfy John's obsessive lust for 'silverware' – winning the FA Cup. Newcastle started their campaign well, winning the third round away match against Everton. In the fourth round, the team were again drawn away, this time to non-league Stevenage Borough. The pitch and the small ground, with a maximum capacity of 8,040, was likely to be their greatest problem and Alan Shearer, after two appearances as a substitute, was going to start for the first time in the season, which was just as well because he scored Newcastle's only goal in a bad-tempered and scrappy drawn game. They went on to beat Stevenage in the replay, followed by victories against Tranmere and Barnsley, both at home, to book a place in the semi-finals.

One interesting, if worrying, statistic was that securing the win over Barnsley was only the third time that season that they had scored more than 2 goals in any game. They did it only once in each of three competitions: 3-2 against Barcelona in the Champions League, 3-3 against Leicester in the Premiership, and 3-1 against Barnsley in the FA Cup. Nothing could more eloquently illustrate the difference between the Keegan approach and the Dalglish approach to management than that statistic!

While the minds of fans and club staff were now focusing on, and looking forward to, clearing the last hurdle before a Wembley final – a match against Sheffield United at Old Trafford – the witch's curse returned with a vengeance the following Saturday. I travelled up to St James' for the game against Coventry, which proved a dispiriting, lacklustre 0-0 draw. After the long journey home, I had barely settled down to a glass of wine and dinner when a distraught Freddie Fletcher rang to tell me he had some very bad news. It was that the *News of the World* the following morning would be carrying an exclusive story, by one of its undercover reporters, running to more than a dozen pages and with the front page devoted to pictures of Freddy Shepherd and Douglas Hall under the banner headline: 'VICE GIRLS SHAME OF TOP SOCCER BOSSES'. I couldn't resist saying to Freddie, 'I thought you said it was bad news?'

Apparently, attempts had been made to serve a High Court injunction preventing publication, but they had failed. Since there were serious implications for the PLC and the club, I asked Freddie to contact the Chairman and the other independent non-executive director to arrange a meeting or conference call on Sunday, by which time I would have read the *News of the World* report.

Unfortunately, neither could be contacted, since the Chairman was in Portugal and John Mayo was somewhere in France. The press, TV, and the fans were demanding an official response. It was a Sunday, so we could delay, but not for long. Given the circumstances, and able to liaise with Freddy and Douglas only through Freddie Fletcher, we arranged to meet Freddy Shepherd in London, where he had gone to escape the media camped around his Newcastle home. Douglas Hall was said to be 'somewhere abroad and not contactable'. Meanwhile, Newcastle United again dominated press, radio, and television news headlines, though it was for all the wrong reasons. Messrs Hall and Shepherd's conduct was inappropriate to say the least and had undeniably tarnished the image and reputation of the PLC and the club nationally. Predictably, it was the mindlessly juvenile insults lavished on the fans, particularly those buying overpriced drinks and replica shirts ('all mugs'), the women of Newcastle ('all dogs') and Alan Shearer ('Mary Poppins') which attracted most attention and caused both hurt and anger.

I met with Shepherd's lawyer in London on 16 March and then again, this time accompanied by Freddie Fletcher and Freddy Shepherd, early on 17 March, advising Freddy Shepherd that there was no alternative to his and Douglas Hall's immediate resignation from all offices at the club. Finally, I met with the non-executives later that morning, after they had returned to the UK. A wave of shock and anger was sweeping through Tyneside, and the Boardroom was no different when I firmly recommended what action must be taken. I was seriously unpopular with all my colleagues on the Board as a result, for a variety of reasons. Sir Terry Harrison, the Chairman, said, 'You had no right to act in such a way – you aren't the Chairman, I am.' Freddy, the culprit, exploded, 'Don't f*****g moralise at me.' And Sir John stated, 'You can't force people who own the club to resign.'

But I argued that there had to be an unequivocal response from the Board if we were to start the process of healing wounds and rebuilding the club's battered reputation. In addition, we were in a precarious 15th position in the Premier League. Dithering now would only exacerbate the problems.

Eventually, after further delays and demands from the Halls and Shepherds, these arguments won the day, with the concession that Sir John could return to chair the Club Board but would not sit on the PLC Board. Yet it was mounting anger from the fans, and hostility in the press, that caused Freddy Shepherd and Douglas Hall to resign.

Amid highly critical press comments accompanied by some savage caricatures of the Board, the club, and its fans, there was a mass demonstration at St James' Park demanding that Douglas Hall and Freddy Shepherd resign immediately. It was also a message carried by the normally highly supportive local newspaper, *The Newcastle Journal*, after the team lost their home match to Crystal Palace on Wednesday 18 March. Anti-Board feelings were running high until at last the signed resignations were published on 20 March. The fans were further mollified by the knowledge that Sir John was coming back. If only they had known how forcefully he had argued for Shepherd and his son not to be forced to resign.

In truth, the PLC Board had been dysfunctional from the outset, with the dominant shareholders free to behave much as if they were still sole owners, after completion of the listing formalities. The procedures of the Board were weak, controls over the subsidiary Club Board minimal, and any serious questioning of plans, actions, intent, or pressure to change met either with evasion, a dismissive response, or a battery of four-letter expletives. Matters had come to a head in a fractious exchange between Sir Terry Harrison and Freddy Shepherd in a shambolic caricature of a Board debate at the Gosforth Park Hotel on 26 February, prior to a Board meeting the following day. The meeting had been called by Freddy Shepherd to discuss a strategy paper he claimed to have written; it had no strategic content. As the arguments between Shepherd and the Chairman became increasingly ferocious, I was asked why I remained silent throughout, which I was told 'was unusual'. I replied that I had no intention of joining in an exchange of expletives that was generating anger and recrimination without progress. Ironically, the Board was disintegrating on the first anniversary of its formation. The Toongate affair, the additional pressure it created and its aftermath, signalled its rapidly approaching end.

Despite these distractions, United had beaten Sheffield United with a Shearer goal to win through to the FA Cup final for the first time in twenty-four years and had concluded their league campaign with a 3-1 defeat of Chelsea at home, followed by a 0-1 defeat at Blackburn, and finished the season in 13th place.

Sir John was still lobbying hard for the two former directors, still shareholders, to be restored fully to the Board, just as the team lost to Arsenal at the beginning of May with the worst team selection imaginable. With the close season to reappraise and regroup much effort would be needed from everybody at the club, from the Chairman to the ballboys, but the problems weren't all on the table yet.

I was boarding a Eurostar train to Paris early on the Friday morning following the Cup Final disappointment when Terry Harrison phoned to advise me that he and John Mayo were resigning from the Board, which I interpreted as purely a statement of their intention to do so. I could sympathise, but responded that I wouldn't be available until Monday at the earliest to discuss it. On the contrary, said Terry, he and John Mayo had already decided, and a press announcement was being issued as we spoke.

All trust had gone in the Boardroom, the performance on the pitch was awful, the fans were rightly dismayed, and I was the only independent non-executive director left. At least I had forged a close working relationship with Freddie Fletcher, the font of most knowledge and the mainspring of action at the club. But, in truth, neither of us had any power to make changes of any significance. It was a board in name only.

The time consumed had been enormous. I had attended twenty-seven meetings in four months since I had returned from Australia at the end of January, while simultaneously chairing two other boards and serving as a non-executive director of another. What more could go wrong before the new season dawned?

With a record of 6 home defeats, 10 away defeats, an aggregate of only 22 goals at home in 19 matches and 13 in away matches, a total of 44 points, and joint 16th place, although 13th on goal difference, the conclusion was obvious. No longer was there a 'Fortress St James', nor was the team a threat to others. They had ceased to be attractive, high-scoring entertainers. Newcastle United needed a strategy, a unified board, and an inspirational manager if they were to avoid relegation and begin the climb to the peaks Keegan had reached. There was less than three months to go before the 1998/99 season kicked off and an impartial observer might have scored the Board's progress since listing, and the club's future prospects, as dismally poor. How, when, and by whom were the challenges facing this once great club to be met?

If that wasn't enough, there were 'Vandals at the gates', and since they were the owners of the club, they were not going to go away. They had to be conquered or appeased.

8

Return to Chaos

My sense of unreality had been enhanced by Kenny Dalglish dedicating the team's FA Cup semi-final victory to the fallen idols – Shepherd and Hall – and was further exacerbated by Sir John's untiring attempts to persuade the Board to reinstate them urgently, so that the club could be run properly! After the resignations of Sir Terence and John Mayo, undoubtedly influenced by these considerations, there was more adverse comment from City financial institutions, questions in football circles, and renewed activity by Sir John. One thing was clear: Hall and Shepherd would have to be allowed to return in some capacity at some time to prevent the collapse of relationships. But the City was as hostile to such a move as Sir John and his followers on the Board were in favour of it.

By July, the position was becoming untenable for me. I was Acting Chairman with no other independent directors to provide a balance, and at a meeting on 15 July, the Board agreed to appoint John Josephs, a well-known local businessman, professional accountant, and lifelong fan, to replace John Mayo. I would replace Sir Terence Harrison as Chairman. Importantly, the Board also agreed to support the return of Douglas Hall and Freddy Shepherd, provided it was only to the Club Board and if it was accompanied by a number of guarantees necessary to secure acquiescence if not enthusiasm from the City. This had taken weeks of bargaining, but the external advisers were adamant that John Josephs' appointment must precede any announcement of Hall and Shepherd's return. This was handled with great care and by the time we had agreed to the appointment of two more 'independent directors', both nominees of the Hall and Shepherd camps, an approved formal public apology by the two men – in which they referred to the scandal as the 'controversial issue in March', and to the consequences of their resignation as 'after which the club had lost some ground' – was published simultaneous with the formal public announcement of their appointment by the company on 24 July. Unsatisfactory? Yes, but the best that could be achieved in the circumstances.

With the new season approaching rapidly, and much to consider, perhaps the club could set aside intrigue and infighting and deal with football matters once again? Certainly, I hoped for this, but the message from an unsmiling Freddy Shepherd in his welcome to fans in a pre-match programme confirmed my doubts. He was by now referring to the 'unhappy incident in March', accompanied by a pledge of commitment to Kenny Dalglish 'every step of the way' and of their 'deep seated love for the club and respect and admiration for those who support it'. One week later, I met Freddie Fletcher and Freddy Shepherd to discuss a replacement for Dalglish, who was said 'to have resigned'. This was how far 'every step of the way' had taken Dalglish after a goalless draw the previous Saturday. The meeting, called at short notice in London before we all went to Stamford Bridge for the match against Chelsea, demonstrated that the successor had already been chosen. Reasons were given. I asked if we had approached Bobby Robson again, but he was said to be 'still under contract'. One week later, for the home game against Liverpool, Ruud Gullit was introduced, with the usual promises of support in the pre-match programme.

I said what I felt – that talented though Gullit was, his appointment again seemed to be driven more by the fact that he was available than by his having the credentials to meet the particular challenge of managing Newcastle United and coping with the ruling clan. After all the usual introductory ballyhoo, he made the worst possible start by losing 1-4 to Liverpool that day and 0-1 away to Aston Villa. As a result, the club slipped to second from bottom. A week later, Newcastle began a run of 3 successive victories, in which they scored 11 goals, with Shearer contributing five of those. They moved smoothly into 9th place, and the city began to breathe again as they went on to secure another victory at home over Nottingham Forest on 26 September to move into 5th place, once again rekindling a flicker of hope that the worst was over.

Yet hope, as always, was partnered by the feeling that something was bound to go wrong. It would almost certainly be self-inflicted. Stirring Boardroom unrest stifled the promise of better things to come on the pitch, this time created by an announcement on the London Stock Exchange News Service that BSkyB was in talks with Manchester United to take over the football club at a premium which valued the business at over £600 million.

Coincidentally, perhaps, there was a formal request from the Newcastle United Football Club Board to discuss future strategy with the PLC Board. This was followed quickly by a series of meetings, including one with the lawyer acting for both Shepherd Offshore and Cameron Hall Developments.

Between these meetings, I spoke privately to Freddy, with Freddie Fletcher present, to tell him that in my view, the issues he had tabled were not the essence of strategy but peripheral matters. I then outlined what I believed our strategy discussions should address, and my reasons for, and the evidence to support, my proposition. I sought his agreement for an open debate of this with both boards, in order to agree on a masterplan appropriate for the next few seasons. He was, as I had suspected he would be, unconvinced. I tried to overcome this by appealing to him on the basis of the likely financial benefits and the probability of the success of the plan, which he dismissed without further consideration.

Game, set, and match to Shepherd. I was genuinely puzzled by his reluctance to hear my views and felt there must be some connection to the BSkyB bid for Manchester United. But, if so, what was it? Rumours of another deal involving a leading Premiership side and NTL, who were seeking to challenge BSkyB's market leadership, were already circulating in the City, as I heard later from one or two of my many City-based contacts. Was the earlier request from the Football Club Board – for which, read Shepherd and Hall – really to seek an endorsement of their plans related to these events, rather than a discussion of football strategy?

If 'a week in politics is a long time' then a month on the Board of Newcastle United was a lifetime. Between then and 17 October, when we entertained Derby County at St James', the club was in crisis both off the pitch and on it as the team slipped down to 10th in the table.

On 14 October, I had been advised by the lawyer acting jointly for the Halls' and Shepherds' businesses that they wished to dispose of their entire shareholding as soon as practicable, confirming rumours circulating in the City during the last few weeks. The scheduled Board meeting on the 16 October, to approve the Preliminary Announcement of Results due to be released three days later, was briefed fully of this late development and the action it needed to consider and, if agreed, take, to protect the PLC.

This also required me to discuss the Board's conclusions urgently with Douglas Hall and Freddy Shepherd to draw their attention to their continuing responsibility as officers of the Club and the need to act in the best interests of all shareholders. Within an hour of the Board meeting closing, I was summoned to meet both men in their office at the ground and subjected to a tirade of expletives, largely by an incensed Douglas Hall, about my interference.

News travels fast in St James' Park. So much for their written pledges of support and regret published in July as a precursor to their rejoining the Football Club Board.

In spite of this, I restated the PLC Board's decision that it should remain in control of any attempt to market the shares in the name of the company. This was also the stance I adopted in the analysts/press briefing of the results, which took place as arranged on 19 October. As the next Board meeting approached, scheduled for 30 November, with the notified AGM to follow a week later on 7 December, it was agreed that we would hold an additional meeting on Friday 27 November to enable Russell Jones, an executive director of the PLC and the club and the Managing Director of Cameron Hall, to brief all Board members on the progress of the stadium redevelopment. Given its cost, this was likely to be the subject of detailed questioning by shareholders large and small at the public meeting. In the discussion, some contentious issues emerged, such as the proposed re-allocation of the season ticket holders' existing seats, to which I, and some other members of the Board, raised objections. When the meeting closed, later than forecast, the company secretary asked to see me urgently to advise me that one minute before the mandatory closing of the list of resolutions to be voted upon at the AGM, a resolution had been handed to him seeking shareholder approval to Douglas Hall and Freddy Shepherd being elected to the PLC Board as directors – to replace John Fender and Tom Fenton if the latter were not re-elected – another self-fulfilling certainty, since a simple majority only was required, which was held by ... well, guess who?

Meanwhile, the team's position was worsening. Newcastle was now in 14th place with only 16 points from its 14 matches. The team had scored only 19 goals and recorded just 4 victories. Alan Shearer had scored only once in his last 9 matches, in which the team had scored more than 1 goal only twice. This decline had started after the Nottingham Forest win in September, which had taken the club to the season's high of 5th place and coincided with the unrest that followed the speculation about a BSkyB/Manchester United takeover.

Don't ever think that what happens in the Boardroom has no impact on a football dressing room. However bad things were, they were likely to get worse. This was a crude and undisguised move by the two controlling shareholders to re-assume full control of the company, Newcastle United PLC, without paying a premium to acquire those shares held by others, which accounted for one third of the shares in issue.

Gone were the pledges of 'democratic rule' made in 1988 in the Magpie Group Charter. Gone were the commitments, made prior to listing in 1997 and repeatedly reaffirmed, not to interfere with the due processes of the Board. Now, in a last act of recidivism, they were, in effect, publicly tearing up the two letters published by both of them only in July – one pledging support to me, as Chairman, and to the Board, and the other apologising to the fans.

However, there was still one last chance to prevent this disastrous slide, and I was determined to do what I could to achieve that.

I spent the weekend consulting with lawyers and other advisers as well as with most Board members prior to opening the Board meeting on Monday 30 November. I briefed the entire Board on the conversations conducted in response to the AGM resolutions submitted by Hall and Shepherd, and on the advice I had received. I told them that my firm recommendation was that we must resist this attempt to regain PLC Board membership, but that before proceeding further, they must individually decide if I should continue to lead the Board as Chairman or quit, which I was prepared to do. The Board was unanimous that I should continue. I therefore proposed to advise the London Stock Exchange, with an immediate public announcement, that the Board had agreed to adjourn the Annual General Meeting set for 7 December and to reconvene it at a later date. I further proposed that, in consultation with the company's lawyers and other advisers, a circular to shareholders to clarify the Board's position and solicit their support should be drafted and issued as soon as possible. This required a further meeting before the formalities of opening and adjourning the 7 December AGM and reconvening it on the first possible date thereafter, 21 December. We finally agreed that a telephone meeting would be held on the following Saturday, 5 December, the last possible date before the AGM. It lasted more than two hours and it was clear that unanimity was unlikely to survive and that John Fender and all three executives were at best wobbling and at worst going to defect. I travelled up to Newcastle on the Sunday night, where I was lobbied to change my stance, which I refused to do. I faced similar pressure from the three executive directors on Monday morning with a request for a Board meeting prior to the AGM, which I also flatly rejected. We then went through the formalities of opening and adjourning the AGM and announcing it would be reconvened on 21 December, before which shareholders would be given a clear recommendation from their Board.

There was a noisy and concerted attempt by some Hall/Shepherd supporters to claim this was improper, which it wasn't, before the meeting was formally adjourned. It was obvious views had changed since the unanimous conviction of the previous Monday, and the Board meeting was going to be difficult.

However, I was unprepared for the demand from Freddie Fletcher, the Chief Executive, for a vote to appoint Messrs Hall and Shepherd to the Board after I had rejected a proposal that we should consider such a move. I reasoned that this was contrary to our publicly announced undertakings and said that in my view it was neither in the best interests of the club nor the minority shareholders and as such was a breach of our fiduciary responsibilities. The company's financial advisers also urged him to drop the proposal. I warned the Board that if a vote was taken and a majority supported the resolution, I would have no option but to stand down as Chairman as my position would be untenable. I reminded him that I had only accepted the role on the written and published confirmation that neither Freddy Shepherd nor Douglas Hall would make any attempt to rejoin the PLC Board and that the Board had been unanimous in its support of me.

John Josephs said that he was in a similar position, having stated in writing that he would only accept the invitation if this was the case and that I was Chairman. Tom Fenton, although a nominee of Shepherd Offshore, said he was in an identical position to John Josephs. The financial adviser present, Martin Purvis, a Geordie and a fan, said his company would also have to resign in these circumstances and advised strongly against the proposed vote.

Despite this, I was obliged to conduct the vote and duly lost by four votes to three. I thanked the Board and left with John and Tom to draft, with Brunswick, the company's PR advisers, an announcement that was issued the following morning. The re-assumption of power was immediate and total and as I left the Boardroom with my two fellow directors I was passed in the corridor by Douglas and Freddy going in, with the latter saying smilingly to me as he passed, 'We all have to lose sometime, man.' Newcastle United was now a PLC in name only, and the ruling junta were back in absolute control of the Board.

On 11 December, Freddie Fletcher, in his new capacity as Chairman and Chief Executive, notified shareholders of the changes, confirming that the Board had immediately appointed 'Mr Hall and Mr Shepherd ... rather than risk a further two weeks of potentially damaging speculation ... They were supported in this by Mr Fender, non-executive director.'

The Board's next announcement revealed to all what this saga, of which they knew but little, was really all about when it announced that the satellite TV company NTL had acquired 6.3% of the company's issued share capital, comprising nine million shares in Newcastle United, from Cameron Hall Developments, who had entered into an irrevocable agreement to sell them the balance of their total holding equal to a further 50.8% of the shares in issue.

It went on to explain that the exercise of this option 'may be influenced by the report of the Monopolies and Mergers commission on the proposed offer for Manchester United'. It made no mention of the fact that the Newcastle United was lobbying hard for free market conditions to prevail in that enquiry or that CHD had banked a little over £10 million already from the transaction.

Had NTL's desire to acquire a stake in the club been met, with shareholder's approval, by the issue of new shares, then the £10 million proceeds would have been banked by Newcastle United rather than Cameron Hall Developments. This money could then have have been available for a strengthening of the playing staff.

Back on the pitch, the season stumbled on with more emergency player acquisitions and no sustainable improvement in performance, except for the solitary uplift of the goals from Alan Shearer that defeated Spurs 2-0 in another FA Cup semi-final at Old Trafford. The league season limped to a close with United in 11th position.

Hopes of an FA Cup win against Manchester United were dashed in an awful display. The Board, the fans, the Manager, and the players were left to reflect on the future as they entered the close season, just as Freddy Shepherd and Douglas Hall were embarking on a high-risk, but financially rewarding, journey.

9

Second Knight –
The Robson Years

Events off the pitch, centred on the revolving door through which the independent directors came and went, had dominated the 1998/99 season, which was also Ruud Gullit's first at the club. Despite having closed with a second successive FA Cup Final appearance, this time against their old nemesis, Manchester United, in May 1999, it had been a disappointment. It had been the first time in nearly fifty years that Newcastle had reached Wembley in two successive years, but the results could not have been more different – 2 stylish wins in the early 1950s, with stunning goals from Jackie Milburn, followed in stark contrast by 2 limp defeats in the late 1990s, without a single goal in either. At the time, I reflected that, because of the eccentric bonus scheme, the players had earned as much by losing as they would have done by winning. This was one of the issues I had tried, but failed, to change more than once in my short time as a director.

After the inherent excitement of the Cup Final had subsided, the majority of fans had rightly focused on the more important fact that Gullit's first season as Manager had not improved the team's league performance. Newcastle had finished in 13th position for the second successive year. True, the team had scored more goals – 48 against the pathetic 35 in Dalglish's last and only full season in charge – but 11 wins and 14 defeats was hardly the stuff needed to excite fans still suffering withdrawal symptoms after the Keegan era. Had that really ended only two years ago? Rumours abounded in Newcastle that there was unrest in the dressing room, that Gullit had not settled on Tyneside and spent more time in Holland than in the UK, and of course that the intentions of the 'trigger-happy' Board were now unfettered – if it had ever been fettered – by a lack of independent checks and balances. But as every fan experiences, the dawn of a new season always brings new and unrealistic optimism for their team's prospects, and in my experience Newcastle fans are better at this than any others.

Some new personnel, the usual public pledges of support for the Manager, and unlimited finance did nothing to cushion the shock of defeat by Aston Villa at St James' Park, accompanied by the even greater shock of Shearer being shown a red card for the first time in his illustrious career. Less than three weeks later, Gullit dropped Shearer for the crucial game at home to Sunderland – yes, Sunderland! Had Gullit taken leave of his senses? The game was played in farcical conditions on a waterlogged pitch and Newcastle lost 1-2 and slumped to 19th place with only 1 point from 5 games.

Rational thought departs at such times, and no citizen of Newcastle, whether or not they were interested in football, felt anything but relief when the Manager was reported to have resigned a few days later. What next? Another much-lauded new face, with the usual platitudes to welcome him? Or someone serious, with credentials to match the need, who could pull up this underperforming squad by its bootlaces and drag them screaming or otherwise to success? Why couldn't the team get back to scoring 70 or 80 goals in a season and to winning more matches than they drew and lost?

Meanwhile, their woes increased as the managerless team travelled to Manchester to be thrashed 1-5. Within a week of Gullit going, a new Manager was installed on the sixtieth anniversary of the outbreak of the Second World War. He was in his sixty-seventh year and he was Bobby Robson, the most successful English manager ever, both at home and abroad. Here was someone who knew how to groom and cope with foreign, as well as British, players. He had managed with great success at Ipswich, and abroad at PSV Eindhoven, Porto, and Barcelona. Now things really would get better, and quickly.

Stubbornly, they did not. A 0-1 defeat at Chelsea in his first match was followed by a resounding 8-0 home win against Sheffield Wednesday, the club's highest score since October 1946, when Bobby and I as boys had separately watched them win 13-0 against Newport County. There were other occasional great days to come, such as when the team defeated Spurs 6-1 in a third round Cup replay at St James', and the storming 3-0 victory over Manchester United, also at home. However, their erratic league form, admittedly with a squad that still bore the stamps of Dalglish and Gullit, meant that they could do no better in the 1999/2000 season than finish 11th with 52 points, although they had scored a more promising 63 goals.

The objective view of the match programme for the FA Cup semi-final at Wembley was honest and accurate. I reproduce it on the next page.

Newcastle
in the spotlight

If the Newcastle United story of 1999/2000 had been broadcast as a soap opera, EastEnders and Coronation Street would have lost out in the ratings war. The events that have unfolded at the North East's most important institution over the past few months have been gripping both on and off the pitch.

Despite it all, they have managed to get towards the end of an extraordinary season with yet another F.A. Cup Final appearance within their grasp. Such a dream seemed inconceivable on that wet night in August when Sunderland slid through the St.James' Park puddles to secure a devastating victory that condemned yet another Newcastle manager to the unemployed list.

Though only three weeks of the season had passed at that stage, there had already been enough events for those script writers to produce an entire series for a soap, with Bobby Robson's arrival bringing about the next few episodes. Whether you have any affection for Newcastle United or not, it has been impossible to ignore a story that will be remembered for many years to come.

Alan Shearer was the name on the back pages after his sending off marked the start of the season and with just one point from their opening five games, it was inevitable that Gullit would depart. The club had openly tried to lure Robson home a couple of seasons before, but they decided to go back for their man and his appointment has proved to be the most inspired move in recent times by the Newcastle board.

If any evidence was needed that Robson had inspired a complete transformation with virtually the same set of players, their emphatic victory over Manchester United last February provided just that. Robson took over a side who had just been handed a 5-1 hammering by the treble winners, yet just a few months later they were more than a match for them. The Newcastle side which started the season in limp fashion simply couldn't have delivered such a passionate and gritty display.

Robson has combined a revival in league fortunes with a great cup run that has been negotiated with just one replay, against Spurs in the third round. His delight at each success has been greeted with a satisfied smile from the man said by some to be too old to accept such a challenge, though no Geordie ever doubted that one of their own would succeed.

They have been to Wembley for the past two years more in hope than expectation that they will end their long wait for a trophy. Victory this afternoon would send them into a third Final with far more belief that they can finally land the F.A. Cup.

KEY MOMENTS IN NEWCASTLE'S SEASON

August 7th Aston Villa inflict a 1-0 defeat on Newcastle at St.James Park. Alan Shearer is sent-off in contentious circumstances.

August 25th Shearer is dropped from the North East derby and Sunderland win 2-1.

August 28th Ruud Gullit resigns as Newcastle United manager.

September 3rd Bobby Robson is appointed as his successor.

December 22nd Tottenham are routed 6-1 in an F.A. Cup third round replay at St.James' Park.

December 28th Newcastle end the year on a winning note at Leicester as relegation fears are banished.

February 12th Manchester United are beaten 3-0 in the North East.

February 20th Tranmere are seen off in the F.A. Cup quarter-finals.

February 26th Shearer scores in a 2-0 win at Sheffield Wednesday and then announces his intention to retire from international football after Euro 2000.

Disappointingly, they were agonisingly close to that third successive Cup Final when they lost to Chelsea in the Wembley semi-final. This was Duncan Ferguson's last appearance in a Newcastle shirt. He had been an expensive failure, costing £7 million, with only 8 league goals from 30 games in 2 seasons. He returned to Everton for half his transfer fee. Would things ever get better? Improvements were emerging, but slowly.

The outlook certainly looked grim when Newcastle lost away 0-2 to Manchester United on the opening day of the 2000/01 season. It was a new season in a new century, maybe, but it was the same familiar result. But the team banished the doom-mongers with some early wins, and were at the top of the Premiership after 4 games.

True, they slipped off the top immediately afterwards, but in an erratically performing league they were in 3rd place by late October, when, after 9 games, they were due to play Everton. Things seemed to be settling into a pattern as Robson tightened his grip and introduced some new faces to the squad. The Premiership seemed to be theirs for the taking, since no team had preserved its 100 per cent record. It was also a week noteworthy for the fact that Kevin Keegan 'blew his top' again, this time as Manager of England when, still in his tracksuit, he angrily announced his resignation to TV cameras in another display of uncontrolled, raw emotion.

United lost again on Saturday at home to Everton 0-1. Alan Shearer's increasing problems in turning defences as he had once done was becoming a serious handicap. He had at that stage scored only three times in 10 matches, and completed his Premiership goal scoring for the season with 2 goals against Ipswich two weeks later. Injury reduced his league appearances in the season to 19 games. He scored his 5 goals in only 4 of those. When he did play, lack of pace and movement had reduced him to impotence in front of goal. With their main goal threat neutralised and the financial brakes on, Robson had a tough task on his hands as the team finished in 11th place with 51 points from only 14 wins, having scored only 44 goals to the 50 they had conceded. Closer examination confirmed the problem. The joint top scorers were Carl Cort, who had played fewer games than Shearer, and Solano, each with 6 goals. Shearer, with 5, shared that distinction with Dyer and Speed.

It was back to the drawing board again for everyone at the club, but for Bobby in particular. His admirers held their breath lest the axeman struck again. Perhaps the executioner's hand was stayed because the fans kept on coming to every home game in droves – an average of 51,039 of them to each game. In the league of average attendances, this ranked them second only to Manchester United. Yes, the money just kept rolling in!

It was a busy close season, marked by intensive activity in order to return key players to fitness. This would be critical to the Newcastle's prospects, since Shearer and Dyer, both of whom had missed many of the final games, entered the close season still having treatment. They were not going to be fit for the opening of the 2001/02 season.

It was obvious that replacements were needed for the short term and that the squad which Robson had inherited had to be pruned and refreshed. It was time for action. Out went Marcelino, Domi, Goma, Cordone, Glass, Gallacher, Hamilton, and Charvet, plus some who had never made an appearance. In came Elliott, Bellamy, Robert, Bernard, and Distin.

Now Bobby Robson could improve the defensive capability, provide a more attack-minded wide midfield, and reintroduce speed to the attack. With all his experience he knew he needed more goals, and that meant he needed Alan Shearer to be fit and scoring freely again. His masterstroke was to reinvent Shearer, but that would have to wait until he returned, which was not until September.

In essence, Robson was determined to use Shearer's undiminished qualities plus his reputation, and to replace his lack of pace by combining him with those who had speed, in order to capitalise on the defensive fears of the opposing defenders. This would turn the weakness he had perceived in Shearer's play into a positive. Translated into action, Shearer would position himself near the edge of the penalty area, shadowed by one or two or sometimes three defenders, Shearer would receive the ball, the defenders would close in, but now Shearer would lay off with head or foot to Bellamy, Dyer, or one of the wide men, which would both loosen the grip on Shearer or allow the pacy young Bellamy or Dyer to exploit the gap.

Shearer's courage, ball skills, and body strength would be used to the full and he would now regain time and space to turn. It was a brilliant piece of creative thinking and man management. However, it couldn't be employed successfully until Dyer returned to partner the increasingly influential Bellamy in the support roles, although Robert, Elliott, Solano, and Speed were playing their part in the developing plan. United had committed to 6 tiring competitive matches in the European Intertoto cup instead of the usual pre-season friendlies, and perhaps in consequence had an uninspiring draw against Chelsea at Stamford Bridge, followed by a similar 1-1 draw at home to Sunderland to take 14th position.

The fans were uplifted, however, by the appearance of Alan Shearer late in the game. His imminent return to league football was signalled by his appearance on the substitutes bench – this time in very different circumstances, although against the same team, to those that had sealed the fate of Robson's predecessor.

Shearer announced his return to something approaching his old form with 2 goals in the next game in a 4-1 win. The team moved up to 7th place, and a week later, still without Dyer, they defeated Manchester United 4-3 at St James' to progress to 4th. With Shearer back and goals being scored, they were able to mount a serious bid for the title. After 3 matches on the bench, Dyer returned to start against Arsenal at Highbury. Newcastle was by then 3rd in the league, and there was a great deal of hope riding on the outcome. They delivered in style with a 3-1 win over the Gunners, including a goal from Shearer, and jumped into 1st place. Better still, it was the start of 6 consecutive matches of scoring for Alan Shearer. The reinvention of their talismanic number nine was complete.

Sadly, their run as 1st in the league was over on the last Saturday of December when they lost to Chelsea 1-2 at St James' to go 2nd. On the following Wednesday, they lost again to Manchester United 1-3 at Old Trafford to slip to 4th, which is how they finished the season on 11 May, but not without a final flourish in February, during which they won all 3 games to temporarily regain 2nd place.

They had enjoyed a very successful season nonetheless, winning 21 games and scoring 74 goals – the highest total they had scored in the Premiership since Kevin Keegan's first glorious season, when they had amassed 82 with only 41 conceded, yet only finished in 3rd place.

Shearer had contributed 23 goals and his supporting attackers had made a major collective contribution – Bellamy 9, Robert 8, Solano 7, and Speed 5 – but United needed to find a twin striker to partner Shearer. The fans were now convinced that Bobby was on the right track and they knew there was much to look forward to as the close season passed. As more changes were made to the squad, there was a perceptible change in the club's approach to the transfer market. The days of a clutch of high-profile, expensive, foreign signings were over; the two most expensive acquisitions were young players Jermaine Jenas and Hugo Viana, both talented midfield players of exceptional promise but no experience at this level of competition. Carl Cort, who had been acquired at the cost of £7 million to replace Duncan Ferguson as a strike partner for Shearer, was seldom match fit after his first season. He only scored 6 goals, but he would have to be retained. The policy was based on cash conservation rather than on building a playing squad which could nurture the green shoots of league success and mount a serious challenge for the title.

The truth was that the squad desperately needed strengthening and the way to do it was not by a policy of 'make do, and mend'. The question in my mind at the time was why was the club – which meant the Board, which in turn meant Freddy Shepherd and Douglas Hall – adopting such a policy?

With revenues from media (i.e. satellite television rights) continuing to grow, sponsorship opportunities expanding, and a rock-solid base of match day cash from 51,000 fans, many of whom were season ticket holders and were therefore paying 'up front' before the season started, there was no shortage of funds if the Board was prepared to invest for success. The potential money and prestige conditional on European Champions League qualification was only accessible through Premier League success, which meant ensuring a position in the top group every year. I kept remembering Freddy Shepherd's dismissive response when I had pointed this out four years earlier. He was quoted in the *Financial Times* several years later, saying, 'You can't run a football club like any other business. I used to drive up that car park, take my business brain out, and leave it on the seat.'

It looked as if that is what he continued to believe! Surely the Board, aka Freddy and Douglas, would see that the club was on the verge of success and riches and that they should now back Bobby Robson to the hilt, rather than the dreaded 'every step of the way' that had presaged the departure of Dalglish!

Many other people shared my view, and perhaps they were fans with influence, because in June 2002, Her Majesty the Queen published her annual Birthday Honours list, which included the name Robert William Robson. Bobby was to be knighted for his services to Association Football.

Newcastle United were to be managed and led by Sir Bobby in the forthcoming 2002/03 season. The portents were good. Keegan's four good years, when Newcastle had finished in the top 6 every year with a 'best' place of 2nd, were now being emulated by Robson's 3rd and 4th places in successive years. I knew and strongly believed that consistently achieving a top 6 placement every year is the platform for success, ultimately to being crowned Champions. It is this consistently high level of performance that attracts top players to the club and provides the financial fuel to afford them, and a regular top four place really does demonstrate that a team has joined the elite.

I will develop this more fully in a later chapter, but for the moment back to the summer of 2002, and to the fans. They had been reassured by 2 very good, if patchy, seasons, and were filled with confidence as well as the usual pre-season hope, further boosted by the shared sense of pride in Sir Bobby's knighthood.

Any reader who finds this strange doesn't yet fully understand the relationship between fan and club, the real sense of shared ownership of the club and its history. If anything, this relationship is more intense on Tyneside than anywhere else I have known and it might help explain, in part, its troubled history.

In June 2002, the mood was euphoric. By August, the talking and dealing were over and United kicked off with a 1-0 win in a Champions League qualifier away to Željezničar. Five days later, they opened the Premiership season at home with a convincing 4-0 defeat of West Ham to go top. Optimism verging on unreality gave rise to false expectations, which were punctured by the end of September when their league position had declined to 11th after only 3 wins in 7 matches. But there was real progress in spite of the recurring setbacks. Jenas and Viana, after starting the first few games, were dropped quickly to the substitute's bench, although Jenas was used at some stage in most of the matches. Lualua was tried upfront with Shearer or as a substitute for him, but was erratic. Yet the supporting forwards contributed more goals and Shearer scored regularly, without ever matching the success of the previous season.

What was more remarkable was that this was being achieved with a squad that was slim and susceptible to injuries. Training facilities were still hopelessly inadequate, which was an ever-present handicap – particularly for players recuperating after injury or surgery. Yet a major investment had been made in ground improvements and St James' Park was ranked high among Premiership grounds. It had the best facilities for players and fans alike, and an attendance record second only to that of Manchester United. It was a strange contrast to the parsimonious approach to team-building and the lack of attention given to the creation of a more robust management structure.

However, the players on the pitch remained motivated, despite a 2-5 thrashing at the hands of Blackburn in early October. Newcastle won their two other league games that month to move up to 9th position. They were 8th by the end of November, 4th by the end of December, and 2nd by the end of January! Heady stuff, but there were warning signs. At the beginning of this run, they had lost to Arsenal 0-1 on 9 November and to Manchester United 3-5 on 23 November. They fell to 3rd by the end of February and held that in March and April, despite a bad month of results when they lost 0-2 to Everton and were humiliated at home by a 2-6 defeat at the hands of their principal rival, Manchester United. Overall, the season consolidated the improvements they had shown in the previous year. But the widespread disappointment, as so often happens, came more from unreal expectations than from failure.

On the other hand, if they had not been smashed by Manchester United in both of their encounters, 3-5 and 2-6, and had not lost 0-1 to Arsenal in November, they might have become Champions with Manchester 2nd and Arsenal 3rd, instead of the reverse. It really had been that close. More serious, objective analysis would have concluded that while such assumptions were premature, the club's progress was real. If properly strengthened by new talent, this squad and its manager were capable of winning the Premiership sooner rather than later.

There were no high-profile international signings in the close season, but there were significant changes in the squad to bolster the attacking power and exploit Shearer's rediscovered menace. Bowyer and Ambrose were young and quick, like Dyer and Bellamy. There was a defensive strengthening, too, in the signing of Woodgate and Bramble. The acquisition of Dyer and Bramble, both from Ipswich, showed that Bobby still had useful talent-spotting links in his old stamping ground. But adding Woodgate and Bowyer to a squad that already included the wayward Dyer and Bellamy was going to exercise Robson's managerial skills to breaking point.

The success of the previous season was also going to impose an early and extreme pressure on the team, as it was now required to kick off the 2003/04 season with a two-leg Champions League qualifying match against Partizan Belgrade, which they lost in a penalty shootout with Shearer, Dyer and Woodgate all failing to convert their spot kicks. This in turn led to more European games as they entered the UEFA Cup, something of a poisoned chalice in that success brought a heavy schedule of extra matches for very little reward. Between the 2 games against Partizan, they opened their Premiership season with a draw away to Leeds and a home defeat against Manchester United. Two more Premiership draws and a defeat preceded their next European game, their first UEFA Cup match, which they won at St James' with a convincing 5-0 score against NAC Breda in which Shearer scored to bring his tally to 6 in 8 games. Bellamy scored twice, while Bramble and Ambrose also scored, the latter making his debut as a substitute for Dyer. Despite these glimmers of hope, there were also early warning signs that all was not well. Once again, the problems were off the pitch. Two days after the UEFA Cup victory, the team flew to London to play Arsenal on Friday evening at 8.00 p.m. They lost 2-3. After the demands of 3 games in six days, a late finish on Friday, and no game until Saturday week, it was decided that the players should have a weekend at leisure, with instructions to report for training as usual on Monday. Most of the players and management team travelled back to Newcastle on Saturday morning.

Given the unusual benefit of a free Saturday, seven players took the opportunity to see family, but two didn't – the ex-Ipswich duo, Dyer and Bramble. There were lurid headlines on Monday of an alleged incident involving seven players in the five-star Grosvenor House Hotel on Park Lane, with allegations of drugs and alcohol and a claim of an attempted rape centring on Titus Bramble and Keiron Dyer. Ultimately, all charges were dropped, but not before a fabric of misdeeds and unacceptable behaviour had been woven by the media into a pattern that condemned all players and the management. While the Grosvenor House Hotel allegations were unfounded, there were some grounds for this in that the behaviour of some players, notably Dyer, Woodgate, Bellamy and Bowyer, had been the object of criticism long before they joined Newcastle. Bobby Robson was also criticised for his 'lack of control', an allegation that was not only unfair, but also lacked any evidence. It certainly didn't help that already, in a season only 9 games old, including the three European games, Newcastle had been the recipients of 18 yellow cards and 1 red card. In the tumultuous weeks that followed, Bramble, one of those under police investigation, was awarded a yellow card in 3 successive games. While the tabloids used every excuse to keep the story running, Newcastle won the next game at home to Southampton on 4 October, as well as the next three against Middlesbrough, Fulham, and Portsmouth, clawing their way up the table to 8th place.

It had been a determined and occasionally inspiring response on the pitch amid the clamour for a 'clean-up' off it, whatever that meant, since the distinction between the responsibilities of the Club the responsibilities of individual players was ignored.

It was onwards and upwards in November. A Shearer-less team succumbed to a 0-5 thrashing at Stamford Bridge, which was compensated for by 4 Premiership games without a further defeat. Newcastle moved up to 7th place, and knocked FC Basel out of the UEFA Cup with wins home and away.

One of the interesting consequences of the game in Switzerland was a reminder that Newcastle United have a dedicated following there. This is partly because Basel, the international hub of the global pharmaceutical industry, is home to a large number of British expats, including my older brother Rex and his family. Sir Bobby Robson was fêted, and thanks to his diplomatically complimentary remarks about FC Basel, both he and United were a 'big hit' on Swiss TV and in the national press.

With the third round of the UEFA competition not until February, the next task was to concentrate on their Premier League performance and build a cushion to offset the pressure of another congested fixture list from February onwards. They couldn't do better than hold on to 7th position in December, although they did contain Liverpool to a 1-1 draw at St James'.

January was another mixed bag of results. After a third round win against Southampton, Newcastle lost a fourth round FA Cup match to Liverpool at Anfield. The team won 2 and drew 2 of their Premiership games, including a goalless draw at Old Trafford, which earned them a move up the table, into 6th place.

February and March were going to be tough, with 5 games scheduled for the short month of February and six in March. With that programme, it seemed perverse to be selling Dabizas, Cort, and Solano, particularly given that injuries had reduced the availability of key players. Cort's appearances in four years had been fewer than Ferguson's, since he had managed to play only once that season before he was sold in January. Bowyer had been unavailable all December and January, Bellamy since early October and Woodgate, who had cost £9 million, from late September to mid-November. Titus Bramble was constantly pilloried by the local paper for his erratic performances and dodgy disciplinary record on the field.

Surely nothing else could go wrong in a club that had only just lost the stigma of the Shepherd and Hall affair and was still living down the Grosvenor House incident? But this was Newcastle United, and more did go wrong, with two unrelated incidents in the fixture-laden February/March period.

The first concerned Alan Shearer. Robson, being aware of Alan's crucial value on the pitch and his desire to play every game, had nevertheless decided to protect him by leaving him out of the away UEFA game against Vålerenga, substituting Ameobi. But knowing Shearer well and anticipating his response, Robson called him in for a chat before that was made known. Shearer was not impressed, but appeared to accept the logic – until United were held to a 1-1 draw, after which, in an impromptu interview with a TV reporter, he made it known that he couldn't understand why he had been omitted.

Since this was the second recent occasion he had questioned Robson's motives and appreciation of him, and both had become public knowledge, they caused a rift, which I believe never fully healed. The original problem had occurred when Liverpool allegedly phoned Freddy Shepherd to enquire if United would accept a bid for Alan Shearer. In the debate that followed, the Manager made clear his own assessment of an unsought approach – essentially, there was no value in selling your principal goal scorer unless you were prepared to invest heavily in a younger scoring ace with a proven record at top level. Somehow, this not only got back to Shearer but also appeared in the press.

The second incident followed hard on the heels of the first. This time it was the *enfant terrible* Bellamy, who consolidated his reputation as a volatile young player with an uncontrollable temper. He had a violent argument with John Carver, a senior coach at the club, which led to chairs being thrown and Carver forcibly restraining him. All of this in an airport lounge while Sir Bobby was holding a press briefing in the next room prior to boarding an aircraft to Majorca for a UEFA Cup match. It also came a week after published accounts of Bellamy's violent behaviour in a Cardiff hotel, when he had been released from a Premiership game against Charlton to appear for Wales. He had undoubted talent, but it came at a price.

Faced with these problems, Robson's ability to control events to benefit the club was remarkable, as was the team's ability to swallow a natural impulse to vent anger on unprofessional colleagues.

In late February, when Robson turned seventy-one, the team were due to return to UEFA action, but first had 2 home league wins and 2 away draws, and lifted themselves to 4th in the Premiership. There was to be no rest now as they began March with the return home tie against Vålerenga, which they won comfortably, with Shearer scoring once and Ameobi twice, no doubt causing both Sir Bobby and Shearer to think this had proved their own differing views after the disagreement caused by Robson's team selection for the previous leg, which had been drawn 1-1.

They went on to beat Real Mallorca twice with an aggregate 7-1 score, and marched into the UEFA quarter-finals. But they were less successful in the Premiership, winning their only home game and losing both away matches to slip back to 5th place. April was a frantic month with 7 games in three weeks. Their winning streak in Europe continued with an aggregate win over PSV Eindhoven, one of Bobby's former clubs, and a 0-0 draw at home to Marseille at St James' before a full house in the semi-final with all to play for in the return leg in May.

They beat Everton and Chelsea and held Arsenal 0-0, all at St James', while away from home they drew with Villa yet couldn't improve on their 5th place because the teams that filled the top four places were Arsenal (who set a record of not losing a game in the entire season), Chelsea (too far ahead on points for the result at St James' on 25 April to have any impact), Manchester United (who took 4 of the 6 points before an aggregate attendance of 120,000 fans), and Liverpool (with whom the points were shared in both encounters).

So, into May for the anticlimactic closing rituals. United drew 3 games and lost one 0-1 away to Manchester City, and five days later lost the UEFA semi-final in Marseilles in a seasonal end that resembled a burst party balloon. Yet they had still finished in the top 6, preserving their platform and consolidating their progress. From this position, they could once more launch an attack on the title next season. The result also meant the club's income improved considerably.

While they finished behind Arsenal, who had amassed 90 points due to not losing a game all season, so too did Chelsea, who in 2nd place were a massive 11 points adrift. Manchester and Liverpool, in 3rd and 4th place, had lost more games, 9 and 10 respectively, than Newcastle had, with their 8 losses. By 3 April, the team had won 12 of their 31 games and had 48 points, putting them in 4th place. But after that date, they only won 1 game, lost 1, and drew 5, scoring only 7 goals and taking 8 points. A clear sign of fixture overload.

That was the problem in a nutshell: they were so close to a permanent position in the top 6, but would only slide downwards without significant, shrewd investment. While that was the core problem, solving it was complicated by bad behaviour on the pitch, which in truth was more a distraction than a difficulty. The real issue was that available funds were diminishing and the Chairman's involvement was not improving that situation.

If Freddy Shepherd and Douglas Hall were intent on pursuing Sir John's dream of a 'Barcelona upon Tyne' they had the example of any of the four clubs ahead of them and the challenge of Aston Villa and Everton behind them.

It was going to be a difficult close season.

10

The Beginning of the End

The usual end-of-season appraisal by both fans and club management was overshadowed by a sense of disappointment. By finishing 5th, United would forego the lucrative glamour of the Champions League for the more mundane UEFA Cup competition. Both competitions brought the same heavy load of extra games, but with extremely different rewards for success. The fans' disappointment was reflected, unusually for Newcastle, by their apathetic end-of-season salute to the players after the final home match. Most of the crowd had already left before the team began the customary lap of honour. Behind closed doors in St James' Park, the disappointment was expressed rather differently. Alan Shearer was grumbling to his manager about the 'unprofessional attitude' of many of the younger players, and Sir Bobby, while agreeing with him, was also reminding Alan that, as club captain, he shared the responsibility for maintaining order and discipline.

Freddy Shepherd had privately enquired towards the end of the season about Sir Bobby's future intentions. Would he continue or retire? Shepherd reminded Bobby that he was, after all, seventy-one years old. Bobby believed that the 2004/05 season would probably be his last full season in charge. However, Bobby also thought that this would be discussed more fully later and that he would be asked to help in the succession planning process. These conversations appeared to Sir Bobby to be nothing more than proper matters for discussion between senior members of the playing and executive management – certainly not the precursors of a major rift. What happened next disabused him of that view.

The first signs came in a call from an old friend in another Premier League club. Bobby's friend told him that Lee Bowyer's agent, having been briefed directly by the club, was touting Bowyer's services around Premiership clubs on the grounds that Bowyer was available on a free transfer. Bowyer was aware of this, and wrongly assumed that it was Sir Bobby who had decided this.

Later, but before the new season started, an interview between Freddy Shepherd and a sports journalist, Michael Walker of *The Guardian*, was published on 31 July. Walker's first question was, 'Will Bobby Robson be staying on as Manager after the '04/'05 season?' The answer was an unqualified 'No.' What followed in the interview was a catalogue of perceived failings, in which Bobby's age was linked with disappointing performances and indiscipline in the club. His transfer record was ridiculed as profligate. Painful and publicly embarrassing as this was, it was exacerbated by a series of Shepherd-led forays in the transfer market, including his being quoted in his favoured medium of the *Evening Chronicle*, prematurely and inaccurately, as saying that Newcastle United were poised to bring Wayne Rooney to St James' Park for a reported fee of £20 million.

When questioned by Sir Bobby about this – and asked how the club could afford this – Freddy told him that he had received an offer of £15 million for Jonathan Woodgate, which would recoup some of the outlay. This was at a time when Robson and he had agreed that an additional centre half was required – hardly consistent with selling United's best central defender. The club also sold Gary Speed to Bolton against the Manager's wishes and without his knowledge, although Shepherd did acquiesce in the purchases of Stephen Carr, James Milner, Nicky Butt, and Patrick Kluivert, though not to Bobby's attempt to sign Michael Carrick, a Geordie who was then playing for West Ham. Bobby Robson, patient though he was, was now marooned, with seriously diminished authority. The earlier problems caused by the mishandling of Liverpool's enquiry for Alan Shearer now resurfaced when new enquiries about his availability came from Souness, the Manager of Blackburn, and Allardyce, the Manager of Bolton, as well as the shock news of the club's pursuit of Rooney for a reported £20 million. Matters were spinning out of control before a ball had been kicked, which Bobby may have unintentionally complicated when he decided to leave Alan Shearer out of the team for a pre-season friendly against Celtic. His intentions were sound and wise – to shield his star striker from possible injury and give new signing Kluivert a warm-up game. But Shearer hated being left out at any time and recent history had given rise to the player's unfounded suspicions of Bobby's intentions. Once the downward spiral caused by the club's leaks, statements, and transfer dabblings had started, a weakened manager was an easy target. On the night before the season kicked off, Robson received a clear indication from Kieron Dyer that he wanted a central midfield role and did not want to play on the right at Middlesbrough. Sir Bobby bowed to the inevitable and picked the newly signed Milner instead. Newcastle drew 2-2, conceding a goal in the last minute. Murmurings began, both inside and outside the club.

Before their next game against Spurs the following Saturday, Bobby sought a meeting with me in private. As I have recounted previously, I had first met him even before I met John Hall in 1984 and although I had not had much contact with Bobby while he was abroad, I had seen him frequently since his appointment at Newcastle on my regular match-watching visits. These had always been informal impromptu chats, mutually enjoyed and informative. This time it was different because he wanted to discuss his position at the club and the sequence of provocative actions by Freddy Shepherd with someone who knew the parties involved and had been around long enough in the upper reaches of business to offer some sound advice. It was also important that we were contemporaries – both vintage February 1933 and fellow Geordies who liked each other. We met at about 4.00 p.m. and talked over tea and dinner until he left at about 10.00 p.m. He was hurt and confused by Freddy Shepherd's behaviour and was searching, not unreasonably, for a rational explanation, repeatedly asking me rhetorically, 'But why do they want me to go, Denis? We've finished 3rd, 4th, and 5th in the last three years. That's the best performance since Kevin. Why?'

I told Bobby frankly that whatever help I could offer he should accept that there was no way back and if the Board wanted him to go then he should seek to manage his exit, if he could, to ensure that he preserved his dignity and reputation. I stressed that there was nothing he or I or anyone else could do to change that – I had been in a similar position at the club in 1998 – if Freddy and Douglas were determined to 'get rid of him'. Yet Bobby still persisted with the question, 'Why?'

Ultimately I told him he must know the answer and we had an amusing yet touching verbal exchange while he continued to deny he knew and I kept insisting he must know. In exasperation, he almost shouted, 'Denis, man, I don't *know*.'

I responded that he should give me the only answer he could think of, even if it seemed too trivial or ridiculous to be true. He thought carefully for a long time and then said, 'Perhaps they are jealous of me but that's really too ... daft! Look what I've done for them ...'

I simply said, 'If nothing else makes sense then however unlikely that seems to you, it could be the answer.' Bobby simply shook his head – he was too honest, too straightforward, to believe Freddy and Douglas could think that way. But reluctantly he did – there was after all no other rational explanation either of us could suggest.

But during dinner, I kept worrying what misdeeds might have been attributed to Sir Bobby and all I could think of were his successes ... *It's you who got a knighthood, it's you the fans applaud and credit with the club's success, it's you who gets the invites to the Royal Box at Wimbledon, and it's you who always comes first when people talk about Newcastle United – but they see it only as their club.*

But Bobby wanted to talk about his problems and I was happy to listen. His preoccupation with what he believed would be an early farewell was supplanted by the need to address the daily problems of a Premiership Manager.

Bobby already knew that they believed he was too old, but they could have said that to his face rather than announce it in the press. They could have said, for example, that to avoid any sudden crisis caused by some unforeseen illness, 'Let's sit down and plan now for your succession,' but they didn't.

He told me frankly of his problems with Dyer, Bellamy, and Bowyer, but felt they were all 'good lads' who were valuable assets but needed firm guidance. He was concerned by Alan Shearer's apparent reluctance to exercise his delegated authority as club captain and his preference to distance himself. Bobby was at pains to stress his admiration for Shearer and constantly extolled his virtues. He never publicly or privately leaked mischievous stories. His attitude was in stark contrast to the deceitful undermining of him by the Board. He remained a gentleman to the end, retaining his dignity in the face of extreme provocation, but behind the public face he was deeply hurt and confused by events. I urged him to try to achieve some temporary accommodation with both Shepherd and Shearer and through this to manage his exit in a more controlled way later in the season, if indeed that was still possible. He was still smiling, talking football and swapping anecdotes as we parted late that evening.

On the Saturday following our meeting, Newcastle lost at home to Spurs 0-1 and for the next match, away to Aston Villa, Robson left Shearer out, picking Kluivert for his first Premier League start. Shearer complained again, Newcastle lost 2-4 and dropped to 17th.

On the Bank Holiday Monday, Sir Bobby was diverted to St James' Park from his routine drive to the Chester-le-Street training ground. There he was greeted by Freddy Shepherd with the words, 'I am relieving you of your position immediately.' This was followed by, 'I am an honourable man and we will honour your contract.'

Amid the seemingly endless coverage this attracted, one simple self-justifying statement made by Freddy has lodged in my memory to this day. When referring to the previous season's outcome, he said, '5th position isn't good enough for this club.' Really? In the 11 seasons they had been in the Premiership, they had achieved a top five position only six times – three under Kevin Keegan and three under Bobby Robson.

The Hall/Shepherd partnership – because nobody else made significant decisions – had managed to disenchant the inspirational Kevin Keegan and to dismiss Sir Bobby Robson, the most experienced and internationally successful English manager to date. The two short-term appointments of Dalglish and Gullitt, characterised by poor results and unattractive football, had separated the two successful regimes.

What they never had was a credible plan aimed at achieving long-term sustainable success, and the creation of such a plan was beyond their collective wit or imagination. After all, it was only 'a corner shop business'. How well did Shepherd and Hall really understand the changing context of top-level football? The only answer is that they didn't. Perhaps they would now reveal what was on their agenda when they revealed why Sir Bobby had been dismissed, presumably with an outline of how and by when the new manager would be required to achieve the improvement on 5th in the Premiership. For the moment, I, like every other supporter, would have to wait and see.

Out went Sir Bobby at the end of August after only 4 games in the new season and even for those fans who did believe that he was too old or had lost his grip – and he knew he had his critics – his public humiliation and sacking was shocking, reflecting badly on the club and all connected with it. Newcastle United had gone from being the great entertainers of English football to being the Premiership pariahs. But Freddy the Chairman did write in his usual pre-match programme notes the following Saturday that 'Sir Bobby and I parted on very good terms. We had some great times together, we remain great friends and I'm sure there will be times in the future when I will beat him again at golf.' Hm … a notch worse than one of his pledges to 'support you every step of the way'?

Who was going to be charged with the task of 'getting this club back to where it belongs as one of the great teams in the world, at the top, and restoring pride and discipline', as Chairman Freddy described the task? Who would want the job anyway? The Board's answer to the Chairman's question was Graeme Souness, who was expensively bought out of his contract with Blackburn, a team at that point 18th in the league. It wasn't long before the football grapevine was festooned with stories of how, if only Freddy had waited, Newcastle United could have saved themselves a few million pounds – Blackburn were rumoured to be about to release Souness anyway.

Whatever his perceived skills were thought to be, they did not work at Newcastle United, as after an early 'dead cat bounce', the team slid remorselessly down the table, finishing in 14th place, which, as often happens in the Premiership, was where they were placed at the end of

December. Worse still, the indiscipline grew worse, its nadir being an 'on-the-field brawl' between Bowyer and Dyer in January, which had already been preceded by well-publicised spats between Bellamy and Souness. One had ended with a physical altercation between the Manager and the player after Bellamy had verbally abused him. Later, after another disagreement, Bellamy walked off the training ground. These incidents led to all three players eventually leaving the club, preceded by the now-familiar self-justifying statements made at intervals over the first few months after Robson's departure by all three decision-makers.

First Sir John, now only rarely acting as the club's spokesman, said on television, 'Bobby should have been sacked after the Marseille game.'

Then Freddy Shepherd, discarding the amicable parting stance adopted in the immediate aftermath of Sir Bobby's sacking, wrote, 'Graeme Souness has been unfairly blamed for what happened in the past week but the seeds of the Craig Bellamy situation were sown before he arrived at the club.' To ensure that this could not be interpreted as a failure at Board level, he also said, 'Many of the problems Graeme is having to deal with are down to the way the previous Manager handled discipline. If Sir Bobby had taken a harder line, I am convinced we would not be facing this situation.'

Douglas Hall was not to be denied his contribution to Sir Bobby's public vilification. In a *Daily Mirror* article, he added, 'We had to get rid of Sir Bobby Robson because he would have got us relegated ... We were going down, make no mistake about it.'

By a strange coincidence, as Sir Bobby was being dismissed in August 2004 – bringing a sad end to his managerial reign after consecutive final places of 4th, 3rd, and 5th, José Morinho, his protégé at Porto, was confirmed as the new Manager of Chelsea. He led Chelsea to the Premier League title as Graeme Souness was taking Newcastle to 14th. The team scored 72 goals to Newcastle's 47. Morinho, the self-styled 'special one', had been brought into the game, initially as an interpreter, by Bobby, the old master, while he was managing Porto. What might have been, given some imaginative, sensitive, succession planning? But that was never an option with this controlling regime.

It was the end of Sir Bobby's illustrious career as a club manager and, as a BBC television commentator sadly said five years later, during the televising of the match between Newcastle and Ipswich on 27 September 2009 – which had been preceded by a memorial service for Sir Bobby at Portman Road – 'It is to the eternal shame of Newcastle United that they sacked Sir Bobby Robson ...'

It is indeed. But when it happened, the end was also approaching rapidly for the presiding trio in the now-beleaguered Boardroom.

11

More Promises, Less Hope, and the Cash Runs Out

The transition from Robson to Souness had been marked by regular comments from the club that things would get better now that there was some 'order and discipline' in the ranks. But it was difficult to see any evidence of that. After all, Newcastle had finished in 14th place, rather than something better than 5th – which was Chairman Freddy's reason for sacking Sir Bobby Robson. Craig Bellamy had also gone in the close season. Whatever benefits that would bring to the team's spirit and discipline, his goal touch and energy would be missed by a team that had only scored 47 goals all season. In 21 matches he had scored 7 of those as a joint-top scorer with Shearer. The sad truth remained that the squad wasn't strong enough and doubts remained about the Manager's ability to change things.

The usual pre-season optimism was soon replaced by gloom as they were knocked out of the Intertoto Cup – which was no great loss, except that the club had sought European qualification by this route.

Spirits were then lifted by another false dawn. The club indulged in an expensive trophy signing – with maximum publicity for the Chairman. Michael Owen was signed in August for a club record fee of £16 million, allegedly against strong counter-bidding, to become the latest in a long line of famous strikers. 'What a partnership with Shearer (9) alongside Owen (10)' ran the promotional line, and soon the tills in the club shops were ringing with purchases of the new star's replica shirts. Sadly, Owen was injured in pre-season training and was unable to start a game until September.

Reality dawned with a 0-2 defeat on the opening day at Arsenal. Newcastle was at the bottom of the table, but the team improved to go 10th by the end of October by virtue of a 3-0 away win at West Bromwich. They were in good company, because at that stage, Liverpool were below them in 13th place while Arsenal and Manchester United were only just ahead in 8th and

7th places respectively. Chelsea were top and stayed there throughout – was this to be a turning point in Newcastle's season? Possibly, since Owen had scored his first goal in September and then his first hat trick on 17 December before breaking a metatarsal bone on the last day of the year. He was out of the reckoning for some months, at least.

With Owen's injuries and patchy performances as a result – and with their talisman, Alan Shearer, now in his last season – Newcastle entered the New Year in 11th position but had a dismal January with only a single point gained from a home draw and 3 defeats. The team dropped to 14th. They promptly lost again on 1 February 0-3 at Manchester City, and on 2 February, as I celebrated another birthday, Graeme Souness was sacked. His record had been dismal too, but the pattern of events suggested that he, like his predecessors, had not been allowed to demonstrate fully whether or not he had the capacity to improve this team's performance. He had inherited a key striker at the end of a record-breaking career, had an expensive, injury-prone successor probably thrust upon him, and had been obliged to discard 'difficult' players rather than manage them. In essence, the Chairman controlled the purse strings while Souness picked up the tab.

Souness had been an expensive import and was now to be an expensive discard. Where could the Chairman find an inexpensive replacement who when discarded, as history suggested he would be, would be just as economical? There could be no more trophy signings, whether managerial or playing staff. The cash cupboard was bare, and for the first time in a decade, the Halls and Shepherds were going to have to forego their joint annual dividend bonanza – now running at over £2.7 million per year. The answer was at home – the Youth Development Manager, Glenn Roeder. He had, after all, been a distinguished player and captain at Newcastle during the 1980s, had recovered from a serious illness, and would be grateful for the opportunity. There would be some criticism from the fans, but Freddy Shepherd believed he was well-practised in handling tricky public relations issues, even though the club still missed Freddie Fletcher's more emollient and accessible presence in such matters. He had been sacrificed after the mishandling of the season ticket holders' seat reallocation following the ground redevelopment, which had caused fans to rebel and the dispute to be settled eventually in the courts. So Roeder it was, but only as Caretaker Manager, with Alan Shearer as his playing Assistant Manager – a sop to both Shearer and the fans.

The club was in a parlous plight and was still in 13th place by the end of March. Relegation was a real and disturbing possibility, with 31 games played and only 31 goals scored all season. Rapid improvement was required, and was delivered in style.

In a glorious April, the team won 5 and drew 1 of their 6 matches in a typically congested month, scoring 15 goals – about half the total scored in the previous 31 games! Unsurprisingly, this spell moved them up to 7th place, with only one game to play, which they drew, to finish the season in 7th.

Meanwhile their companions in mid-table in October, Manchester United, Liverpool, and Arsenal, had also improved to finish 2nd, 3rd, and 4th behind the season-long leaders and reigning Champions Chelsea. The problems were blindingly obvious. No club would ever be Champions if they didn't score more than the 47 goals Newcastle had scored in each of the last 2 seasons, with the club's key goal scorers low in the table of successful Premiership strikers.

In 2005/06 Shearer was United's highest scorer with 10 goals but only ranked joint 17th in the Premiership table, while Ameobi with 9 goals was 18th and Solano with 6 was 53rd. Michael Owen, in an injury-dominated season, had only been able to contribute 7 goals – expensive ones, given his £16 million price tag! That the fans hadn't relinquished belief in the club was evidenced by the fact that the average attendance at St James' was consistently over 52,000 during a less-than-satisfactory season for the second successive year.

Roeder had also persuaded most fans that the team's exciting end-of-the-season finish entitled him to the position of Manager. There was no reason to delay – other than the fact that he was not qualified to be a manager under UEFA rules. Roeder's qualification course had been rudely interrupted by a serious illness some years before, but after his full recovery, he was now back on course for early completion. That technical hurdle overcome, Roeder was duly appointed Manager on 16 May as the season ended.

Alan Shearer retired and his replacement as Assistant Manager was Kevin Bonds, a former colleague of Glen Roeder at West Ham. Almost immediately, there were allegations in a *Panorama* programme of 'bung taking', including by him during his time at Portsmouth, and his contract was terminated. Controversy and scandal were now, it seemed, an everyday occurrence at St James' Park.

Newcastle United again entered the Intertoto Cup as a prelude to the 2006/07 Premiership season and went on to surprise most people by winning it and gaining European qualification. Obefemi Martins joined from InterMilan but even with his recruitment, Shearer was now gone and Owen's fitness was a major worry, so it was difficult to see where Roeder could find the goals needed to get remotely near the league leaders.

Owen had only played 30 minutes in the penultimate game of last season, but he had trained hard, declared himself fit, and was picked for England's World Cup squad in 2006. In the game against Sweden on 20 June, he was badly injured, sustaining cruciate ligament damage, and was not fit to play again for United until April 2007. It was a hammer blow for Roeder before the league programme had even kicked off.

Poor Roeder. While Shepherd and the Newcastle Board raged against the FA and demanded compensation for the loss of Owen, his salary burden, and the cost of replacing him, the Manager had to get on with the job. It was an uphill task as the team slipped down the table, recovering slightly in December and then strongly during a good January, in which they won 2 and drew 2 of their 4 matches to move up to 9th. Repeating the now-familiar pattern of results – which should have influenced the Board but clearly didn't – the end of January also marked the end of the pack shuffling for 1st place as Manchester United confirmed they were fireproof, Chelsea similarly in 2nd, Liverpool in 3rd, and Arsenal in 4th – places that they all retained to the end of the season. When was 'the penny going to drop' for the Board? The practice of random trophy signings to appease fans was no substitute for building a competitive team, any more than the random sacking of managers was going to provide direction, and the Chairman's frequent dabblings in the transfer market were unlikely to attract or support professional managers. Few people thought Roeder would survive, although the majority knew who the real culprit was. Surely enough, Roeder was summoned to an emergency board meeting after a 0-2 loss at home to Blackburn following which his resignation was announced, and he departed with only one game of the season left. How insensitive could this Board's behaviour be to treat a decent man, who had been dealt a terrible hand by them and fate, like this?

One week later, Newcastle finished their season in 13th place with 38 goals – of which Martins contributed 11, Dyer 5, and Ameobi 3, and they were the only Newcastle scorers in the top 100 Premiership players for the season. The team's goal tally of 38 was 45 fewer than Manchester United's 83. How were Newcastle going to address this if they still harboured the belief that they could prove to the footballing world that Freddy Shepherd's declaration, 'Newcastle United, one of the greatest teams in the world', was more than self-delusion?

I agreed with the objective, though not with their process, and it seemed to me it would require a long list of earthly miracle workers, a team of Houdini, Dick Barton, James Bond, and Indiana Jones to achieve it. But there was a more cunning plan than this, and the first clue to what it might be appeared in a surprise managerial resignation on 29 April 2007.

Sam Allardyce, whose Bolton side had finished ahead of Newcastle, had surprised his own board by resigning, declaring that he had taken Bolton as far as he could. About three weeks later, having met Freddy Shepherd in London on 15 May, he was appointed Manager of Newcastle United. He replaced Glen Roeder on 21 May with a three-year contract.

Hardly had that news been digested when it was overshadowed by an announcement on 23 May that 'SJHL, a company owned and controlled by Mike Ashley, had bought 55,342,223 shares in the company – Newcastle United PLC – representing 41.6% of its issued share capital.' This was followed on 6 June by the announcement that 'SJHL and the Company have reached agreement on the terms of a recommended offer for the entire issued and to be issued share capital not already held by SJHL'.

Deals of this kind are not agreed on the same day as they are announced, so it is a reasonable assumption that Freddy, Douglas, and Sir John knew of this long before they sacked Roeder and recruited Allardyce. They also knew that the company was virtually insolvent and that they needed to get out quickly or see their investment unravel. They cashed in their chips for over £92.5 million, while both Freddy and Douglas, as serving directors, were paid more than £1 million each in compensation 'for loss of office', which, together with the benefit of their remuneration of £500,000 for the year, meant they walked away with pay for the year of over £1.5 million each.

They left behind a club in financial meltdown, Newcastle's reputation as an exciting, attractive, entertaining football team in tatters. They also left the hopes and dreams of maybe hundreds of thousands of Geordies trampled in their rush to exit. Where had the lofty words and aims of the Magpie Group that Sir John had written in 1988 gone? 'To democratise the club.' 'To revitalise the Board.' 'Together we can make Newcastle United the focal point for revived morale throughout the North East.' Surely they had not been forgotten? Sadly, the agenda changed as soon as the dream was within reach – i.e. in 1996, when Keegan's team was close to achieving the club's first senior Division title in seventy years. This was when Sir John and his Board decided to seek a quotation on the London Stock Exchange. Nothing was ever the same after that.

An empty feeling was felt keenly on Tyneside – a feeling of being let down, of being conned by the empty promises over so many years. But pessimism never lasts long in Newcastle. They had heard it all before and they knew it could all happen again, but the chat soon turned to, 'What do you know about this fellow Ashley?' Hope springs eternal in the human breast, and they would soon find out – after all, a new season was due to start. 'Mike Ashley couldn't be worse than Freddy and Douglas though, could he?'

They were soon to find an answer to that question, too.

12

New Owner, New Season, New Manager, Same Problems – Only Worse

When it was announced in June 2007 that Mike Ashley was the new owner of Newcastle United, the 'required' resignations of four Board members – Douglas Hall, the Halls' tax accountant, and two other representatives of the Shepherd and Hall families – followed later in the same month. Freddy Shepherd stayed on for another month before he too resigned at the end of July. As a consequence of Ashley's newly formed company, SJHL, acquiring Newcastle United, it sought and achieved the cancellation of its listing on the London Stock Exchange. Fans immediately fell into the familiar trap of thinking that matters must soon improve, if only because they could not get any worse than they had been recently. They were about to find out exactly how inaccurate such an assumption was.

Very few people knew much about Mike Ashley other than that he was a very wealthy businessman; even fewer seemed to know why he had taken an interest in acquiring Newcastle United or if he had been aware of the imminent appointment of Sam Allardyce during his negotiations with Sir John. He was not a Geordie, and, apart from products he sold in his sports shops, he did not appear to have any connections at all with football or Tyneside.

He immediately unveiled his new Chairman: Chris Mort, a well-known corporate lawyer from a major City firm, who was to be supported initially by two non-executive directors. The club, it appeared, was going to be run in a very different way now, more in the mould that Abramovitch had successfully introduced at Chelsea than the failed model the Halls and Shepherds had adopted.

The best news of all appeared to be Ashley's ability and willingness to get the cheque book out and 'splash the cash'. There was a clearing out of the less successful players, and in came some new reinforcements.

Between June and the transfer window closing in August, Newcastle signed Barton, Rozenhal, Viduka, Geremi, Alan Smith, Capacca, Enrique, Faye, and Baye. Out went Boumsong, Parker, Bramble, Srníček, Bernard, Sibierski, Moore, Dyer, Solano, and Luque. It was comprehensive but was it being done to balance the books or to build a title-challenging side? Were these choices made by Ashley or Allardyce? Or by some other member of the mysterious Mr Ashley's entourage who had not figured in the public announcements to date? These were only some of the intriguing questions being aired throughout Newcastle before the new season kicked off.

While there was nothing new in pre-season speculation and the airing of hopes and fears for the months ahead, there was undoubtedly an added frisson this year, simply because there was a new owner after a seventeen-year reign by the Halls and their junior partners. At the time, though, the big unanswered question in most minds was this: is Ashley's wealth, obviously so much greater than that of the Halls and Shepherds combined, going to be used to match the financial muscle that Chelsea, Manchester United, and Liverpool's new foreign owners had invested with such success? Would it enable United to compete with these teams on equal terms?

The season kicked off on 11 August, coincidentally away to the new Manager's old club, Bolton. The new owner had already discovered that the anonymity and ambiguity that had shrouded him previously was being rapidly exchanged for constant exposure under the glare of Premier League floodlights. The previous owners had courted that exposure; the new one had to learn to live with it, and there are few places in the football world where those lights shine more harshly on failure than at St James' Park. The sun shone brightly for every one of the Newcastle contingent that afternoon, except for Michael Owen, who was absent through injury yet again. United strode to a 3-1 victory. Not only was it a good omen, it seemed to be endorsed by a string of good results. Michael Owen returned for the home game against Aston Villa one week later, a draw. By mid-September, Newcastle were 5th in the league, and the team hadn't lost a game. Owen scored his first league goal for Newcastle since December 2005 in their win over Wigan, and with the next game away to Derby, who were at the bottom of the Premiership and already looked destined for relegation, further progress up the table for United seemed 'odds on'.

Hope really was growing with Chelsea behind Newcastle, Liverpool only one place higher, and Manchester City in 3rd, already breaking the Big Four's monopoly hold on the top four places. More than sixty years of watching Newcastle United had taught me not to readily extrapolate current success to forecasts of certain victories for succeeding games, but even I was shocked when they lost 0-1 away at Derby, the only win Derby achieved in the entire season – during which they scored only 29 goals, conceded 89, and mustered only 11 points.

Humble, inadequate, disorganised Derby became Allardyce's *bête noire* that year, as you may remember. Morale slumped, and fears, replacing early optimism once again, grew that the earlier success was no more than a 'flash in the pan'. But another impressive run of 3 wins, in which they scored 3 goals in each, offset by the single 1-3 defeat to a better-placed Manchester City, helped restore faith in the new regime. Newcastle were now in 8th place, with 17 points after 9 games and with a game in hand over Chelsea and Liverpool, who were both ahead of them. If United could win that game in hand, they would leapfrog both and then, notionally, be in 4th place. Yet they somehow managed to lose away to Reading, a team that would later be relegated alongside Derby. After this match, Newcastle hit a disastrous, season-condemning patch of bad form, during which they lost 4 games and drew two without a single win, scoring only 5 goals and conceding 14.

Although they were then in 11th place, it was clear that there was little prospect of a top 6 position, while the manner of their defeats at Derby and Reading was an indicator of serious underlying problems.

True as always to their history, the players shook themselves up by winning the next 2 games, one of which was a less-than-convincing 2-1 victory at St James' over Birmingham, who were to end their season as the third relegated club. But that was enough for the fans to approach Christmas with a better heart.

Seasonal entertainment for the fans would involve a home game on Saturday, carol singing and festivities on Sunday (which was Christmas Eve), and games away on Boxing Day and the last Saturday of the year. A game at home on 2 January would open the New Year and the second half of the season. All that was needed was a consistent performance to get the team close to European qualification.

The team soon dampened those Christmastide expectations with another pathetic display against Derby. It was a 2-2 draw; the visitors were gifted 4 points from their two meetings. What a rotten start to the holiday programme. Worse was to follow; they lost the next 3 matches and as a result their 'new Manager', Sam Allardyce, suddenly became their 'previous Manager' after less than eight months. Newcastle were a not-unreasonable 11th place in the league, with 26 points and 17 games still to play, but that was a massive 24 points adrift of the leaders Arsenal. More worryingly, it was only 9 points better off than Sunderland, then in the third relegation spot. The immediate question now was who could

Ashley and his team identify to ensure survival and begin the restoration of a battered club?

Certainly I revisited my own doubts about how, why and by whom Sam Allardyce had been recruited. The Board of Newcastle, at the time of that appointment, was presumably aware of Sir John Hall's negotiations with Ashley, and the likely outcome – a takeover of the club. In addition, however, I, and certainly Mike Ashley, given his business interests and the quality of his corporate advisers, knew something of the scale of the emerging global financial crisis, which was causing concern when the season opened and which was clearly going to get much worse. Context and timing is everything in business, and this certainly seemed to be a business deal for Mike Ashley. Everyone was taking a financial hit and for some it would be terminal, as it was to be for Northern Rock, the club's principal sponsor, soon to be renamed 'Northern Wreck' by local wags. How typical of Newcastle United to be able to claim one of the largest, most prominent, and earliest of the UK banking sector failures as their biggest financial sponsor. Against the possible effects that a macro-economic collapse would have on his extensive business interests, Ashley now had to find an immediate micro-economic solution, given that he had breached Allardyce's three-year employment contract and had to woo a new manager, as yet unidentified, to pick up the pieces after the latest in a growing line of sacked managers stretching back decades. In a crucial period of the season, when final positions were being determined and relegation was still a threat, this was neither the easiest nor the most welcome of tasks. It was difficult to believe that Ashley would undertake this task personally, nor that his appointed Chairman, Chris Mort, was any better equipped to do it either. But who else was there? High-profile vacancies with no clear succession breed rumours, and we were all to have our fill. While rumour and counter-rumour swirled, manager-less Newcastle travelled to Old Trafford and were humiliated in a 6-o thrashing by the Premiership Champions designate, who by the end of January had displaced Arsenal at the top and were now on a charge to the title! Poor old Newcastle, poor Ashley – what else could go wrong?

Remember that he is, and probably always will be, a retailer at heart. He did what any good retailer would do in such circumstances. He shopped for someone the fans would find irresistible, so that whatever went wrong afterwards, he, Mike Ashley, would nevertheless remain in their 'good books'. He unveiled not a new Manager but an old hero, King Kevin, popularly and irreverently known as 'The Messiah'.

I was besieged with calls asking for my view on the great news and my response was an unequivocal, 'Sorry, it was the right move seventeen years ago but it's the wrong move now and it will end in tears.' One well-informed source reassured me that it would not, because Keegan was going to have an equally heroic Assistant Manager, Alan Shearer, who in two or three years at most would become the Manager. Kevin 'would move upstairs' to become Director of Football. I have no idea if that was wishful thinking on his part or a serious intent, but I pointed out that in my view Shearer would not accept the post of 'Assistant' to anyone at Newcastle and those who suggested otherwise had no idea what made the man tick. Whatever had been planned and negotiated in the wake of Sam Allardyce's sudden departure and the defeat at the hands of Manchester United, Kevin Keegan duly signed a contract on 16 January 2008, for three years plus the remainder of the '07/'08 season, which still had 16 games left to play. He was paraded before his still-adoring fans, for whom he could no wrong despite the frailties he had revealed during his managerial career since he last left St James' Park eleven years ago. Within two weeks, Alan Shearer had publicly rejected any question of his either being offered or rejecting an Assistant Manager role, stressing his TV commitments.

While this was still hot gossip, another fatal error was made in the announcement that Dennis Wise had been appointed as an executive director at a rumoured salary of £1 million per annum. The new owner was prepared to spend readily on his own perceived solutions, but he could have had no inkling of what the average Geordie football supporter thought about that appointment. Worse still, it rekindled their memories of one of John Hall's most intemperate outbursts, in which he promoted his concept of 'Geordieland' – the enemies of which naturally lived in the south. Still, there was more than a hint of a southern bias in the decisions made at St James' Park – which appeared on Tyneside to be lacking sensitivity to the aspirations of the fans, who were bonded by a blind love of Newcastle United, a central part of their culture for more than a century. The seeds of another tragedy were being sown already.

More objectively, and given my insider knowledge of the club and its ways, I feared that my misgivings about the Keegan appointment were going to be proved correct much sooner than I had anticipated. Yet somehow this unholy alliance held together until the end of the season.

King Kev had not yet proved to be the miracle worker some had unrealistically expected, and United eventually finished the season in the same lower half position he had inherited.

His record of 4 wins, 5 draws, and 7 losses in 16 games was somewhat worse than that of Allardyce, but it was Allardyce's squad and most notably Keegan knew he had to improve his strike force if Newcastle was ever going to challenge for honours again. No doubt he was looking forward to demonstrating to his admirers that he had not lost his magic touch, while I was wondering if Ashley would bankroll Keegan's ambitions now as John Hall had done initially all those years ago.

It was going to be a busy close season and perhaps a really exciting new 2008/09 season. The Premiership was scheduled to open with an away fixture at, of all places, Old Trafford, against the reigning Champions. Keegan going head-to-head with Ferguson in the lions' den, after that humiliating defeat in the interregnum of January, was a match to die for. There are no easy games in the top league, but this one would be more difficult than most. Off the pitch, local press gossip hinted at what most feared – that Keegan's wish list was not being followed and that the new appointees at the club, Wise, Jimenez, and Vetere, were probably driving the reshaping of the squad and the transfer plan, if there was one, during the close season.

Nevertheless, Newcastle came away from Manchester with 1 point after a good 1-1 draw and beat Bolton at home 1-0 the following Saturday. It was a good start to the season, but the following Saturday the whole edifice collapsed due to three different shockwaves. It all centred on the game at Arsenal on 30 August, the season's third league match. The first happened because Mike Ashley had adopted the practice of shunning the Directors' Box at both home and away games to sit with fans wearing, as they did universally and to his obvious delight, a replica United football strip of black-and-white stripes. Initially, this had been welcomed by fans and greeted as a novel, friendly gesture by 'the Boss', but that had now begun to grate. On this occasion, Ashley took things too far by carrying a pint of beer with him. When challenged by stewards, he said that it was non-alcoholic. Since non-alcoholic beer was not sold in the ground, this appeared to be a wanton breach of ground regulations, and Ashley was cautioned. Newcastle lost the match 0-3 to complete an unhappy and deeply embarrassing day for Mike Ashley.

The second shock came later when Keegan, in a radio and television interview, made clear his desire to build a better attacking side. During his answers to the questions which followed, he also made it clear that it hadn't been his idea to sign Xisco or Gonzalez. Contrary to rumour, he repeated that James Milner was definitely not for sale. Milner, he said, was an essential part of his plan to build for the future.

Privately, Keegan was furious to think such a plan was even being considered without his knowledge. Ashley was even more furious when he heard Keegan's outspoken responses in the interview. Shortly afterwards, the transfer of Milner to Aston Villa was completed for a fee of £12 million.

The sequel was inevitable, and precisely as I had feared and forecast. Keegan had a blazing row with Llambias and Wise before storming out of the meeting. He had gone, never to return. Ashley, at first believing Keegan's needs would cause him to cool down and accept that he was powerless to change some things, stood off until the venom of the crowd turned on him. This was unpleasant, unwanted, and damaging. He appears to have instructed his team – Wise, Llambias, the Chief Executive, and whomever else was involved – to 'fix it', and fast. But Keegan couldn't be pacified, and in the absence of reconciliation, lawsuits were instigated by both parties.

Perhaps that was inevitable anyway, given Keegan's angry departure and the other issues which had surrounded the fateful defeat at the hands of Arsenal and which had combined to threaten Newcastle's dreams – yet again! Inactivity encouraged this to fester in the absence of a league match for two whole weeks. By the time the team had emerged from the tunnel on Saturday 13 September, everyone was desperately hoping for a shaft of light to chase away the gloom. After all, they were still in 9th place with 4 points, and Hull City, the visitors, were one place behind with the same number of points. Surely United would win ...

But this was Newcastle United, with a long history of self-destruction, and they lost ingloriously and humiliatingly for Hull City to go 4th and Newcastle to drop to 15th. The team had lost more than their manager; they had lost direction, motivation, and morale.

13

The Witch's Curse
Revisits St James' Park

The row on Tyneside reached storm proportions, and Ashley, now rocked as he had never been before, announced on the following day, 14 September 2008, that he was quitting and putting the club up for sale, three weeks into his second season as owner. It was only two weeks since he had been cautioned for his behaviour while dressed as a Newcastle United fan, and it was ten days after Kevin Keegan's public resignation. In Newcastle United's long and frequently stormy history, those two weeks almost certainly rank as the all-time low, brought about by a series of calamitous, ill-considered actions and responses by everyone, in a cast of thousands. No one, from owner to management to manager to players to fans to media, could escape criticism. Mike Ashley's unprecedented reaction was more than the angry response of a rejected and vilified billionaire – it was abject surrender to a superior opposition, the collective fury of the fans. It demonstrated that no one had been able to help him understand the depth of the relationship between fan and football team.

His public statement was unambiguous. 'I have listened to you. You want me out. That is what I am now trying to do.' Perhaps he had also forgotten the importance of context and timing. In an economic recession, it is easier to buy than it is to sell. This problem could not be excised by surgery or eased by medication. He was going to have to learn to live with the pain for a little longer. For how long, no one knew.

Yet another promise, yet another golden dream, had been shattered, this time more quickly and explosively than ever before. Could this ill-tempered and damaging rift be healed, or was the club now terminally damaged? This was the question on everyone's lips.

It is difficult to exaggerate the feelings of hurt, anger, rejection, and helplessness that hung like a shroud over the city. The remorse at lost dreams, the perplexity of being abandoned by an owner the fans had welcomed little more than a year ago, and the overarching feeling of helplessness were inevitably expressed in angry public outpourings. As always, the media gleefully seized on a really interesting opportunity to carry a 'bad news story'. This tendency fed on itself and grew to ridiculous proportions.

The loss at the Emirates Stadium in August had been Newcastle's first of the season, but it had exposed all the frailties and flaws of an ill-conceived management plan. The furore simply increased as the team lost the next 3 games before they managed to stem the slide but only with 2 high-scoring draws before yet another defeat – at Sunderland.

At the end of September, with 6 games played, Ashley's team had identified a new Manager, the experienced Joe Kinnear. It was unfair to him, but hardly unexpected, that the fans greeted his arrival with disbelief and derision. He was seen as a good workman but unlikely to inspire the players, or indeed the fans. The appointment reignited doubts about the selection process, since Harry Redknapp had also been seen visiting the city, but had turned down the opportunity to manage United. To the fans, both Redknapp and Joe Kinnear were 'Londoners', for even though Joe was Irish, it was his time as a player with Spurs and as Manager of Wimbledon that had pigeonholed him as a 'cockney', as was Dennis Wise, who in their eyes had created many of these problems. The fans discussed this endlessly in pubs and clubs, which they believed was where such incongruous appointments must have been decided. Whatever was going to happen in the rest of the season, this, in retrospect, was the point of no return. It wasn't only the fans who were unconvinced by Joe Kinnear's appointment, for within days he was embroiled in a furious exchange with sports writers. He lost his temper and swore serially throughout his interviews. It was an unpromising start, with echoes of previous misdeeds, and a reminder that Joey Barton, a misguided signing by Allardyce, was still in prison.

In the wake of the Emirates Stadium row, the storm continued to rage for weeks, and never fully abated. It was reminiscent of the anger that was vented on Freddy Shepherd and Douglas Hall after their antics with call girls in a Spanish brothel and their alcohol-fuelled ramblings about Geordie women, fans' gullibility, and Alan Shearer's domesticity were made public. It might have reassured Mike Ashley that Shepherd and Hall survived and prospered financially even though it seemed to be terminal to their future at the time. The most visible sign of the shock Ashley had suffered was in his absence from games. What most incensed fans was that newspaper column inches were filled with the latest rumours of who was negotiating with Ashley's men to buy this once-great club at a bargain basement price.

The season dragged on with the relief of a victory, Joe Kinnear's first, against West Brom. This was at the end of October, and was followed by his second, a few days later, against Villa. Newcastle then had another bad patch of 5 matches without a win, before another 2 wins moved them up from 17th to 12th place. They suffered yet another dreadful run of 4 defeats and 2 draws in 6 consecutive games, by which time it was February and they were 'staring down the barrel', and it wasn't a beer barrel either. On 7 February 2009, they were in the Midlands for their match against West Bromwich Albion when cruel fate interfered again and Joe Kinnear was rushed to hospital after a heart attack, which ultimately required major surgery. That was the end of his sad season, which had been dominated by pressure and adversity.

Newcastle won that day to record a double over West Brom, which was of little consequence, since they were below Newcastle in the league. It was only Newcastle's sixth win of the season, but surprisingly they were in 13th place with 27 points after 25 games but a massive 27 points behind the Premiership leaders, Liverpool.

Chris Hughton once again took up the reins as Caretaker Manager. He led a dispirited, injury-prone squad that struggled through another 5 games, of which two were drawn and three lost. Two of the defeats were at home and since they were against what most Geordies saw as their natural rivals for honours, Manchester United and Arsenal, it was salt in open wounds. Ashley knew he must have one last desperate throw of the dice with only 8 games to play and United in 18th position and relegation bound. Knowing the workings of retailers' minds rather well as I do, his next move was totally in character and reminiscent of his ill-fated choice of Keegan the previous season! To put that into context, remember what had gone before – it explains a great deal.

Little more than two years earlier, Ashley had achieved the greatest triumph of his life. He had achieved a stock market listing for the company he had created at the age of nineteen with one shop. He had built this business into a retail sports empire with several hundred outlets and a stable of top-quality global brands epitomised, for me, by Dunlop and Slazenger. That London Stock Exchange listing crystallised his business's value at £1.9 billion on 27 February 2007, and since he retained two-thirds of that, he had a personal wealth, on paper, of well over £1 billion. Less than three months later, he had, apparently suddenly, swooped on Newcastle United PLC by buying Sir John Hall's personal holding for approximately £55 million. He completed the acquisition of the company in a few weeks. The move had the hallmark of a retailer's gut feel for a signature transaction.

With the novelty of knowing the extent of his vast personal wealth, he appears to have regarded this as a 'petty cash' purchase without the safeguards of a 'bog standard' due diligence review. It was an expensive error, but it was no more than a retailer's gamble that hadn't worked yet, but could. Less than two years later, it had turned out to be part of an uncomfortable series of reversals that had seriously diminished his wealth and reputation. The world's financial markets had gone into free fall and Ashley's Sports Direct empire was then worth a fraction of its original value. The reasons for his recent acquisition of shares in some of his competitors had attracted the attention of the Office of Fair Trading and media comment. His speculative investments in other stocks like the Royal Bank of Scotland had resulted in substantial losses, and Newcastle's principal sponsor, Northern Rock, had been nationalised and was unlikely to be able to renew the expensive contract – which would have less value if the club was relegated. Instead of becoming a local hero, wearing his own personalised football shirt, swapping stories, and drinking beer with the lads, he was now public enemy number one.

It was time for his retailer's instinct to be given full rein again, which he did by appointing Alan Shearer as Manager, perhaps unwisely on 1 April, with only 8 games left to play. Shearer was made in a very different mould to Joe Kinnear, and drove a hard bargain. He would accept the job only until the end of the season, and review his position then. This was typical of the stance he had adopted on the field, where ruthless single-mindedness had helped create the goal-scoring star of European football. The appointment endorsed the rumour that Shearer had been asked to partner Kevin Keegan the previous year; his refusal had only increased the asking price.

The Shearer obduracy had one other immediate consequence. Newcastle announced that it had 'released Dennis Wise'. The retailer's touch had the fans dancing in the streets again. 'Big Al will do it. Howay the lads,' was the cry ringing in the streets. There was hardly a glance back at the litter of broken pledges, the opportunities squandered, the crushing of Keegan, the insults of the 'Toongate' scandal, and the sacking of Bobby Robson. Football fans are readily forgiving – or perhaps they are die-hard fantasists.

For the moment, however, a happy truce reigned and everybody breathed more easily ... until 5.00 p.m. on Saturday 4 April, when Newcastle trooped off, having lost again 0-2. It was against Chelsea, reasoned the disappointed fans. In the 28 games played since Keegan stormed out, the team had won only five times. The last of those victories had been against fellow strugglers West Brom two months previously. They drew another 2 matches and lost another 2 before Shearer managed his first win, 3-1 at home to Middlesbrough. To the fans, it was a glimpse of safety, of escape from relegation.

In reality, it was meaningless, just like the 2 wins over West Brom, a team who were, throughout the season, below Newcastle in the league. With only Fulham to play at home and Aston Villa away, United were now dependent on other teams losing. With only 7 wins in 36 matches thus far, victories were statistically unlikely.

I was, above all, a long-suffering fan, and there was only one place I had to be on Saturday 16 May and that was St James' Park. I wanted to catalyse the same miracle I had 'performed' seventeen years earlier, to avoid relegation, and to start the march to glory ... Or so I had persuaded myself. I had my friend and ex-colleague Freddie Fletcher invite me to the ground for lunch and to his seats in the Directors' Box, where the conversations were full of apprehensive speculation.

We met up with my old friend Sir Bobby, who looked very ill but sounded, as always, optimistic and determined when I asked him how he was feeling. He smiled, shook my hand, and said simply, 'Still fighting, Denis, still fighting.' Newcastle lost again, thanks to a disputed goal after they had already had a similar score disallowed. It was the kind of cruel fate that seemed to follow United around. As I was leaving the ground an hour or so after the end of the match, I saw Sir Bobby again, this time being taken in a wheelchair to the lift, where we stopped to have another chat. After a short exchange on the game itself, he looked me in the eye and said, steadily, 'You know Denis, if you had still been Chairman, me the Manager, and Freddie the Chief Executive, this would never have happened.'

'This', we both knew, meant relegation, the one word neither of us wanted to use but which we knew was virtually assured. It was the last time I saw Bobby before he died on 31 July, by which time the dream we had both harboured of a golden future and for which both of us had worked in our different ways, had already died, confirmed by a further defeat at Aston Villa on 24 May.

This is where we came in, and where I began this review of history, and of the last twenty years in particular. Before I turn to the question of why it all went wrong and what should have been done, let me conclude the story as Newcastle set out to escape from the Championship. They had to do so quickly to avoid succumbing to the fate of Leeds, Sheffield Wednesday, Queens Park Rangers, and other teams which have never regained their lost Premiership status. Frankly, Alan Shearer's appointment was yet another error by Mike Ashley. His readiness to do the job was always a matter of doubt, and the fact he would only commit to 8 games before reviewing his position was not the answer the desperate situation demanded, however happy the appointment made the fans.

Neither did Shearer's experience match the need, and this showed in some of his selections. He persisted with Owen, endlessly repeating that he would score goals, which Owen didn't. This seemed driven more by protecting a member of the 'England Centre Forwards' Union' than by a willingness to make the tough choices that managers must make in difficult situations. His own resentment at being left out of the occasional starting line up had preordained his approach. An inadequate squad with fading morale was an extremely difficult situation for him to take on; most successful Premiership managers have learned their craft long before they take on such a level of challenge. Nobody should do so for only 8 games.

His record was worse than his predecessors'. Compare Shearer's 8 games to the 30 played before his arrival:

	P	W	D	L	GF	GA	P
Before Shearer	30	6	11	13	36	49	29
With Shearer	8	1	2	5	4	10	5

Newcastle United ended their 16th consecutive year in the Premiership in 18th position and were relegated with only Middlesbrough and West Brom below them – these teams had provided Newcastle with 10 of the season's meagre total of 34 points. Those statistics, together with a total of 40 goals all season, pinpointed both the problem and the potential solution.

14

Champions Again, and Hopes Run High

The close season of 2009 was unlike most others in that the squabbling and rancour of a defeat-ridden season continued to fester. This is quite different to the usual close season atmosphere, for supporters throughout the land tend to sow fields of dreams every year for the forthcoming season and expectations grow while those dreams assume a cloak of reality as kick-off day draws nearer.

But not on Tyneside this year. There was simmering anger throughout May, June, and July, and the intense dislike of Mike Ashley and his entourage was exacerbated rather than diminished by the summer break from action on the pitch. Away from the stadium, Shearer appeared to be trying to negotiate better terms to continue his unsuccessful management reign, Joe Kinnear remained nominally the Manager on sick leave, while Chris Hughton was doing his best to get on with a difficult job.

Behind the scenes, yet somehow also simultaneously on the sports pages everywhere, news appeared with ticker tape continuity of possible new owners ranging from a consortium of Arab Sheikhs to another of Americans to, nearer home, a consortium in which Sir John Hall was involved and a cut-price bid – what else? – was made by Freddy Shepherd. Yet the most likely candidate appeared to be another local businessman, Barry Moat. However, it was clear from a very early stage in the negotiations that he did not have the financial muscle or the ability to raise additional funds to complete the bid, even though it appeared that Ashley, in his desire to be rid of this now poisoned chalice, was prepared to offer deferred terms.

The fans were delighted that Moat was on the scene. Why? Because he was a local man from a family that had successfully run a business in Tyneside for many years, and he was a genuine long-term fan.

Slim credentials perhaps beside those of Mike Ashley, but had it taken fans only 2 seasons to forget what damage the last local owners had wrought? The answer, undoubtedly, was 'yes'. Even as this non-stop diet of news was being digested, the new season kicked off on 8 August with an away fixture at the Hawthorns against their fellow relegation sufferers and leading contenders for promotion, West Bromwich Albion. The game, played before 23,500 people, was a less-than-enthralling 1-1 draw, and the teams were shown as joint 8th in the league table that evening. Newcastle then reeled off 3 consecutive victories without conceding a goal to move smoothly up to 2nd place and, after a win in the Carling Cup over Huddersfield, they went on to beat another promotion contender, Leicester City, again without conceding a goal, to take undisputed 1st place on the last day of August. It was a great start for Chris Hughton, the team, and the fans. The latter were still lukewarm, even with this record, and attendances were very low by historical standards, only once exceeding 40,000, and only 24,000 for the Carling Cup game. Hardly surprising though, given the opponents the team had faced and the fans' hostile attitude towards the absentee owner.

Meanwhile, Barry Moat was still actively trying to garner support for his takeover of the club. More stealthily, the old 1988 Magpie Group Charter was being dusted off and refreshed by another set of local aspirants under the new banner of 'NUST', or the Newcastle United Supporters' Trust.

With no league games scheduled for the first weekend in September, Newcastle resumed their strengthening campaign mid-month with another clean sheet, winning by scoring the only goal at Cardiff to remain top of the Championship. There was cause for concern as well as confidence, because in 4 of 6 games, they had scored only once, simply not good enough for a stranglehold on the title.

As if to emphasise that, they lost a few days later at Blackpool, scoring only once yet again, enough to fall to 3rd place before another sparse crowd of under 10,000. Carroll scored his first goal and followed that with another in a 3-1 home win a few days later at home to Plymouth, moving the team up to 2nd to reclaim one of the two automatic promotion spots. To complete a topsy-turvy week, they travelled to Peterborough for a third round Carling Cup tie and lost 0-2 before a crowd of 10,000, failing to score for the first time in 10 matches. Like the United of old, they bounced back against Sir Bobby's old team, Ipswich, with their highest score of the season, winning 4-0. It was an emotional day for everyone. The pre-match ceremonies included a memorial tribute to Sir Bobby every bit as moving and impeccably observed as the formal memorial service held in the grandeur of Durham Cathedral, which had been a few days earlier. He would have been touched by the fans setting aside petty rivalries to celebrate a much-loved giant of the English game.

The victory also took Newcastle back to the top, but the self-congratulation was premature. They finished September with 2 draws, one of which was 1-1 at home and the other scoreless. Bad, yes, but worse was to follow. They suffered 2 away defeats, one of which was to the much-fancied Nottingham Forest. However, they only fell one place, as most of their nearest challengers were stumbling at the same time.

Two key questions arose for management to answer because of these results. The first, as I have already highlighted, was how to build a strike force capable of scoring 2 goals per game on average? The other was how to motivate a team to play its heart out on lousy pitches in a dilapidated stadium before a handful of spectators? The defeat at Scunthorpe on 20 October again attracted only 8,921 of them, fewer than often accompanied United on their travels in the Premiership.

On the following Saturday, they beat Doncaster 2-1 at home before almost 44,000 fans, their highest gate of the season, to regain 1st place, with goals scored by Nolan and Carroll, the seasoned pro and the novice, who became the leading scorers throughout the season, as the goals per game ratio increased.

Chris Hughton seemed to be tightening both his grip on events and his grasp of how to sustain progress. Perhaps his positive response to adversity was infectious, because Mike Ashley, after an expensive settlement following arbitration of his public dispute with Keegan, terminated the futile talks with Barry Moat and on 27 October he announced that he was abandoning the search for a buyer. He went on to commit himself to the future success of the club – he was, he said, now focused on achieving promotion and promised a further cash transfusion to strengthen the team. Great stuff, and exactly what most fans wanted to hear, especially as he went on to express regret for having made serious errors of judgement caused by a lack of knowledge of what football club ownership was really all about. Refreshingly honest and welcome, perhaps, except that he went on to first confuse and then to upset them all over again, by announcing that he intended to sell the naming rights for the stadium. 'What,' the unspoken question went, 'a different name for St James' Park?' Worse than that, as he revealed on 4 November, it was to be renamed sportsdirect.com@St James' Park Stadium.

The wafer-thin sensitivities of the long-suffering diehard supporters were exposed, yet again evidenced by their outraged reaction. Sportswriters and football commentators used this as an excuse to introduce a comedic element into their reporting of Newcastle's growing dominance of the Championship title race. Perhaps it was this that caused the recently formed NUST to 'come out' in a very public way, claiming in its first online newsletter to have 'launched the most ambitious campaign undertaken by Newcastle fans, with emails to 40,000 magazines, press coverage in thirty-seven countries, and thousands of pledges of support'. Its more extravagant claims included the reassurance that 'the principle of one investor one vote ... meant ... if you invest the minimum amount or £100 million you get the same voice'. Really?

Whatever the real level of support, its timing was as unhelpful as its motives were misguided. More importantly, as all began to realise grudgingly, Mike Ashley demonstrated his conversion to their cause through results. Chris Hughton and his team completed another sequence of 6 wins, during which the team conceded only 1 goal, yet scored 12 to increase their lead at the top to 7 points, with only a match away to Barnsley before they were faced with the crucial, intensive Christmas programme.

But they could only draw that game, unusually conceding 2 goals in the process, before normal service was resumed with a convincing 2-0 win over Middlesbrough before a 50,000 crowd, the biggest of the season despite the wintry conditions that gripped not only Tyneside but the whole country. United's lead was now 10 points. Yet as Christmas brought more snow, ice, and falling attendances, both perhaps contributory factors, the players' form deserted them.

In an awful sequence of three league and three FA Cup games, they drew four, lost one, and won only one – a Cup replay against Plymouth before less than 16,000, the lowest attendance for a Cup tie at St James' for ninety years. It proved to be a meaningless victory anyway, because they were dumped out of the Cup in the fourth round by West Bromwich Albion only six days later. They needed to regroup and reassert themselves. They were, after all, still leading, although with a reduced lead, but the latent threat from West Brom was emphasised by the result. Their patchy away form continued through to mid-February with drawn games at Leicester and Swansea, capped by a 0-3 defeat at Derby, knocking them off the top of the Championship. It brought back memories of how Kevin Keegan's team had surrendered the Premier League title at a similar stage in the season a decade ago. However, a more rational appraisal – does that ever apply to Newcastle United? – would have given due weight to the fact that they had held an automatic promotion spot continuously since 19 September and were only 2nd on goal difference, with a game in hand. Surely they would be promoted, probably as Champions? Everyone could then return to the big issue of whether or not Mike Ashley really wanted to remain or if he could be persuaded to do so. And if not, who else could bring a more settled, perhaps triumphant, future?

So it proved to be, at least as far as the promotion issue was concerned. The team collectively banished any lingering doubts with a string of 11 games without a defeat, of which they won eight to enter the Easter programme with a lead of 6 points over the nearest challenger. On Easter Monday, Nottingham Forest, then in 3rd place, failed to score in their afternoon home match, thus losing their slim chance, if only a statistical one, of qualifying for an automatic promotion place by displacing Newcastle United. The St James' Park crowd of just fewer than 50,000 celebrated in appropriate style before Newcastle's evening game kicked off. The team, despite going behind to an early goal, went on to win.

A smiling, unusually subdued Mike Ashley was present to get some pleasure without a trace of hostility – no more than his due reward. Minds could now be concentrated on the certainty rather than the possibility of a return to life in the Premiership and all that implied.

Two games, in the sharply contrasting venues of London Road, Peterborough, on Easter Saturday, and St James' Park a week later against Blackpool, reinforced the need to prepare for a different scale of challenge. Peterborough's ground is small and the playing surface was uneven and bare, with more mud than grass. A sell-out crowd of almost 13,000, disconcertingly close to the pitch, the familiarity of the home team with the pitch conditions, and the unfamiliar crescendo of noise, much of it from the visiting Toon Army, combined to give Peterborough a great boost and an early lead as Newcastle endured an uncomfortable first half. They were unable to find their passing rhythm and couldn't cope with Peterborough's speed or the barrage of high balls behind the midfield, yet they equalised on the stroke of half time. Some substitutions, a goal from a perfectly executed free kick, and a rapidly tiring home side gave Newcastle a hard earned 3-2 win, which paved the way for the early celebrations on Easter Monday. The following Saturday showed the contrasting face of the Premiership, in the home game against Blackpool at St James' with an impressive, packed stadium of 50,000, providing a beautiful playing surface on which any team capable of doing so could play fast passing, attacking football. Newcastle did, and recorded a 4-1 victory.

But the lesson was clear. You have to play one way to get out of the Championship and then abandon that as soon as possible, reassess the squad, and decide what must change and how to do it, in order to survive and prosper in the Premiership.

As I travelled back to London that evening, I kept remembering that May day eighteen years previously, when Newcastle had avoided the drop to the Third Division while those clubs safely in the First Division were preparing for life in the new Premier League, due to kick off in August

1992. Now, having regained their rightful place and having missed only 2 of the 18 Premiership seasons, the club must do a better job than they had done between 1993 and 2007 of responding to challenges both known and yet to emerge.

The owners throughout that period, the Hall and Shepherd families, had left behind a trail of broken pledges and a club that was virtually insolvent. Successful managers and players had been discarded; scandal and disunity had plagued this once-proud club. The paragon had become the pariah. Now a fresh start could be made with an owner who seemed to have learned from his initial mistakes and had already invested some £250 million to acquire and maintain the club. His relationships with the fans had been fractious and the fans had been vociferous in their support for local initiatives, such as NUST, which sought to wrest control from Ashley. If Mike Ashley had admitted his mistakes and achieved what many thought improbable in the swift return to the Premiership, then surely they could reciprocate and accept that he had earned their support from now on?

I also replayed in my mind a few memorable soundbites heard during this season.

- **Football commentator, September 2009:** 'It is to the eternal shame of Newcastle United that they sacked Sir Bobby Robson.'

- **Announcement by Newcastle United, October 2009:** 'The Club has confirmed that it has been withdrawn from sale and is no longer on the market. Mike Ashley stated that he is totally committed to the future success of Newcastle United and will be focusing on gaining promotion back to the Premier League. Mike will put a further £20 million into the club this week.'

- **Article on Freddy Shepherd, 'The Oligarch of the North-East', in the** *Financial Times*, **February 2010:** 'You can't run a football club like any other business. I used to drive up that car park, take my business brain out and leave it on the seat.'

Meanwhile, the season was to conclude with one more point added to Newcastle's tally, removing even the statistical improbability of West Bromwich usurping them for the title, thanks to a draw against Sir Bobby's old team Ipswich. With this, Newcastle achieved a new club record – an unbeaten home record, and it was the only club to do so in all leagues in the 2009/10 season.

They duly achieved both, to crown a wonderful season. Success brought increased attendances, nudging 50,000 for every home game and increasing enquiries about season ticket availability – both signs of a softening attitude towards Mike Ashley.

Now all that remained was for peace to break out in Newcastle; for the fans and the whole community to support the present owner in recognition of his and the team's achievement. It was time for reconciliation.

If Mike Ashley followed with action rather than empty promises, another Golden Era could ensue. The 2010/11 Premiership season might just be the start of this. Do I believe it can happen? Yes, of course!

You see, once a fan, always a fan.

15

The Open Letter to Mike Ashley, June 2010

Dear Mike Ashley,

First, congratulations on Newcastle's achievements last season. Most fans' highest expectations would have been met by achieving promotion this year, but to do so as Champions, by an even more convincing margin than Kevin Keegan's great side did in 1993, signals a return to the Premiership with great confidence. You and the team are all due our thanks, support, and respect.

As a football fan all my life, and a Newcastle fan at that, having been born and formed there, I have watched the decline of this great club in recent years with sadness rather than anger and I couple this with sympathy for you.

As a businessman with a great deal of experience in retailing, I know that you will have faced problems very similar to those you are now facing at Newcastle United many times before, and that in the process of building your Sports Direct business from a single outlet to its present impressive scale, you will have needed optimism, resilience, and skill to achieve your goals. It is these qualities you now need to call on.

My sympathy is because you inherited a severely damaged business, weakened by incompetent handling over a period of years, for which you, surprisingly, overpaid.

The Newcastle fans, and indeed the majority of the local population, welcomed the change of ownership initially because the club's decline was keenly felt locally, and in the process they invested you with the responsibility of fulfilling their long-cherished dreams of success by swiftly returning it to the upper reaches of the Premiership. That was unrealistic on their part, but that's the way fans behave and think. All football club owners must recognise that.

They are not unique in this, as recent outpourings of dissatisfaction at more successful Premiership clubs such as Manchester United and Liverpool have testified. That they should do so is partly attributable to the fact that they are not just customers, whether they are season ticket holders or pay at the turnstile.

Because they invest so much of themselves in it, they feel they 'own' part of the club, they respond to the team's victories with pride and to defeats with sadness. Whatever happens, they can't take it back when it lets them down and exchange it for another football club, as they can with a tennis racquet or a bag of golf clubs. It is part of them and they are part of it. They dedicate so much of themselves to Newcastle United and yet they have no power to change things other than by exhibiting and articulating their frustration.

Voting with their feet by non-attendance is simply not a realistic alternative for most of them.

I feel sure that you, too, know that you have made some serious errors in your choice of personnel and structure which, sadly, combined to break the bond of trust with the fans.

There is a jewel of a club hidden in the garbage of recent history. This club can be returned to its former glory and you would not only be rewarded financially but you will have replaced the hurt and anger fans feel with a genuine sense of gratitude and pride.

I hope you too feel it is not too late and that your decision to retain ownership can be transformed into a commitment to restore the club rather than take an expedient and temporary step. If you do retain the club's ownership you have the skills, the power, and the funds necessary to achieve that longed-for success. That is what everyone seeks – actions not more empty promises – and when you do take that step it will finally be the day that the promises stopped and success was delivered.

Through the club's recent achievement, you have taken a giant step towards regaining that trust. You can go on to greater things – if that is what you really want to do. I hope so. However, if you have not read this book yet, I urge you to do so. I feel sure you understand that exhilarating though the 2009/10 season has been, life in the Premiership will be 'a whole new ball game' – if we are to avoid history repeating itself.

I wish you well and, given time, I hope that all Newcastle fans at home and abroad will do so too.

Good luck,
Denis Cassidy.

16

United's Return to the Premier League 2010/11

The atmosphere on Tyneside during the close season returned to the normal pre-season optimism despite the nationwide economic gloom casting long shadows over incomes and employment

I was preparing to launch the first edition of this book in which I included in Chapter 15 The Open Letter to Mike Ashley, June 2010 and the continuation of the Newcastle United story. In that letter, which was never acknowledged, I urged him to read the book because I had used Newcastle United's history to illustrate what could be done to avoid the mistakes of the past to his, the club's and the fans' benefit and pleasure. In effect he and the team had collectively done the 'hard part' by their swift return to the Premiership and whilst I was prepared to adopt his 'wait and see' policy before making further major investment in strengthening the squad, that did not mean the current squad would be able to achieve more than survival, at best, in that league.

There must have been a sharp intake of breath at the club when the fixture list was published with the opening game away to Manchester United on 16 August – this would indeed be the ultimate reality check. Before a crowd of 75,000, Manchester strolled to a 3-0 victory. Welcome back to the big time! However, there wouldn't be any tougher opponents to face and the following week United entertained Aston Villa and, perhaps because the game was televised, they rampaged to a 6-0 victory with the previous season's top scorers, Carroll and Nolan, sharing 5 of those. Disappointingly only 43,000 fans attended whilst millions watched on television and were impressed. Their next game was away to Wolves, which ended in a 1-1 draw and after a two-week break they faced Blackpool at St James', a side promoted with them that season. It was Blackpool's first-ever season in the Premiership, they had lost 6-0 on the opening day and hopes were high on Tyneside that United would repeat their own thrashing of the same opponents last season. A 50,000 crowd saw Newcastle lose 0-2 in a limp display and although they unveiled one of their new signings, Hatem Ben Arfa, who looked very promising, the doubts about the team's collective ability to survive, let alone prosper, at this level surely re-emerged in the Boardroom.

Yet hope was re-kindled only a week later when they travelled to Everton, who had held Manchester United to a 3-3 draw the previous week. Ben Arfa scored the only goal, an impressive second new signing, Cheick Tiote, made his debut, as did Tim Krul, a young Dutch goalkeeper to replace the injured Steve Harper – all three new boys seemed destined to make a big impression in future. A good win and three talented newcomers – perhaps pre-season optimism was justified after all? But, this is Newcastle United and seldom is that the case as 2 successive defeats, by Stoke City and Manchester City, followed by a nerve-racking 2-2 draw at home against lowly Wigan, demonstrated. Even more worrying was that Newcastle were losing 0-2 at half time and only a goal by Coloccini in the 94th minute saved a point! Equally true to form and history United then reeled off 2 excellent away wins in London, 2-1 at West Ham and 1-0 at the Emirates, and between those games outplayed Sunderland winning 5-1 at St James' before 52,000 people and watched by millions more on TV. They were then 5th in the Premiership with 17 points from 11 games, only 3 points less than the 3rd placed side! With Carroll and Nolan back on the score sheet regularly, was this to be that season defining point? Alas no, for they then struggled through a sequence of 5 games without a win and added only 2 points to fall to 12th. That, in retrospect, really was the season defining period despite the fact that Andy Carroll had won an England cap and scored regularly. But in the last of those defeats on 5 December at West Brom, the only Newcastle goal was scored in injury time by a substitute.

The following day the Manager-without-contract, Chris Hughton, was sacked. He had outperformed a string of managers who had attempted to retain Newcastle's Premiership status and failed ... he had regained that status in his first season. Did he deserve to be sacked after only 16 games? Or, if the sacking was thought to be justified, what were the justifiable grounds? That there were some difficult first team players was beyond doubt, that those members of the 'awkward squad' included three of the most talented was also true, but I had a lingering doubt over the wisdom and timing of Hughton's dismissal. If it was really a case of his perceived failure to deal with talented, wayward players which had led to his abrupt sacking, was he alone to blame? Would sacking him cure the problem? I, like most other true fans, was in turmoil

– the gathering pace of United's assault on a top 6 place had come to a juddering halt. Why and by whom had this had been triggered was followed by other questions of who, why and when will the successor be named? Within forty-eight hours of Hughton's dismissal, Alan Pardew, a former player and like his predecessor recently sacked, by Southampton, was appointed. To bring the whole episode to a tidy conclusion within the week, Newcastle defeated Liverpool 3-1 in Pardew's debut with a side that contained all three troublesome players – Carroll, Barton and Nolan – and all three scored before a full house of 50,000!

While questions went unanswered, Newcastle lost to Manchester City at St James' and then to Tottenham 0-2 after which rumours started to surface that Carroll's departure was imminent. Alan Pardew vigorously denied the rumours with the time-honoured response 'We are looking to add to the squad ... Carroll will be here as long as I am here'. Carroll never played another game in the famous black-and-white stripes and it was symbolically the last match of 2010. Coincidentally the opening of the transfer window was imminent. In his absence the team opened the New Year with 9 games of which they won 3, drew 5 and lost only 1 in the process climbing back to 9th but, with 36 points, now below Sunderland. In the middle of this run Carroll was sold to Liverpool for a reported £35 million to replace Torres who, in a back-to-back pre-arranged deal, had been transferred to Chelsea for £50 million.

This run of games throughout January and February had brought a welcome 14 points, an indication of stability rather than success. True United scored 15 goals without Carroll but 9 of those came in 2 home games – the 5-0 demolition of West Ham, who were relegated, and the extraordinary 4-4 draw against Arsenal after being 0-4 down at half time. Closer study of this run shows that in 6 of the 9 games United either didn't score at all or scored only once. The total goals scored, 15, were contributed by Best (5), Nolan (3), Barton (2) and Lovenkrands (2) with Ameobi, Tiote and Coloccini each scoring once. Anyone who looked beyond the headlines would have shared my doubts about what might happen in the remaining 10 matches of the season because this strike force was patently below the required Premiership standard.

Only 2 games were played in March and both were lost with only 1 goal scored (by Best) against 6 conceded with the 2 winning sides, Everton and Stoke moving above United, who in consequence fell to 11th place. After another two-week break Newcastle were at home to Wolves, yet again relegation candidates. A 50,000 crowd was there to re-invigorate them, which they did as United gained a precious 3 points in a 4-1 win to start the final stage of the season on 2 April. Sadly it was another false dawn as the remaining 7 games produced only 1 more victory, defeating

Birmingham 2-1 who were subsequently relegated, 4 draws and 2 defeats. A grand total of 7 points in 7 games, which is relegation form! In 3 of those games United failed to score.

Two of the drawn games are worthy of further comment for very different reasons. The first was a scoreless draw at St James' at Easter against Manchester United, the eventual Champions, who in the season scored 78 goals. But the second, the final game of the season, again at St James' on 22 May showed the least attractive and most worrying aspect of Newcastle's performances. It was against West Bromwich Albion with whom they had tussled in the Championship race for promotion last season. It appeared to have been a consequence of defeat by the same team in the away match in December that Chris Hughton had been sacked. So there was much to play for as United launched themselves into attack before a baying capacity crowd of over 50,000 and after ending the first half leading 2-0, increased their lead immediately after the break to 3-0, courtesy of an own goal by West Brom. The crowd was ecstatic but they had overlooked the fact that a game is at least 90 minutes long and after scoring in the 62nd minute West Brom scored again in the 71st before finally equalising in the last minute of injury time. The crowd had suffered through successive stages of anticipation, pleasure, ecstasy, rapture and fantasy only to slide down the slopes via concern, anxiety, grief and finally, to anger. Such is the life of a football fan and unsurprisingly some of the crowd booed as a crestfallen side trooped off the field. What would have been a nerve-racking 3-2 win had at the death ended as the squandering of a 3-0 lead. Little wonder it became known as 'Suicidal Sunday'.

It was as they angrily left the ground that fans began to question seriously what lay ahead for their much loved team, who really made the big decisions and what really were the owner's objectives? One thing was certain, a tortured close season lay ahead. What a transformation in a mere twelve months.

17

Promises? What Promises?

The words used by J. S. Blatter – or Sepp to his many old pals in FIFA – in response to criticisms of his reign as President of FIFA, 'Crisis? What crisis?' This caused me to ponder how Mr Ashley (call me Mike if you are a season-ticket-holding, replica-shirt-wearing Newcastle fan) might respond to a similar question.

How strange that another football season has just ended, in a two-week period of glorious achievement for some, and irredeemable disaster for others, but more likely somewhere in that 'no man's land' between and yet, here I am already focused on August. Yes, the start of yet another season due to stretch through autumn, winter and spring to close in May 2012! Why not first enjoy summer and all its other sporting events? Or fly off to sun, sand and sea somewhere and just forget about football for a few weeks? The simple answer is that I can't. I would like to, but I can't and I suspect if you are reading this, neither can you! So what follows is my thought process and if reading it you are relieved, I will be delighted. On the other hand if it causes you more concern than you felt previously, join the club. Any views about the future must begin with an assessment of the season 2010/11 just ended together with a review of expectations when it opened and of the significant events during it. It is above all a fan's-eye view and judgement, against which you can test what you felt at the same stages.

During the close season of May–August 2010 I was about to publish the first edition of this book which included The Open Letter to Mike Ashley, June 2010. In that letter I expressed the hope that his, then recent, apology and declaration of long-term commitment to the rebuilding of a once-great club, allied to the outstanding season we had all enjoyed in winning the Championship and promotion to the Premiership, could be used as a firm base on which to build.

I was prepared to give him time to add 'financially prudent' signings selectively rather than indulge in the crowd pleasing trophy acquisitions of his predecessors. Yet I stressed that nobody should expect even the outstanding Championship side Chris Hughton had assembled to conquer the Premiership in the coming season but they might achieve what I argue in the same book is Newcastle's rightful place. That is, in the top 6 most years and the top 12 in a very poor year. The logic for that is set out in the book which I urged Mr Ashley to read even if Mr Shepherd had rejected it a decade earlier.

Against that background, what were my expectations?

First, that the Caretaker Manager, Chris Hughton, would be confirmed as Manager and a contract signed to lock him in. That did no more than recognise that he had made a major contribution already while his development and future would be discussed with him. His responsibilities would be covered in the contract which would charge him with delivering a plan based on his perceived player needs consistent with the Board/Owner's declared financial targets.

Secondly, that a review of the playing staff and costs would be discussed and agreed with Chris Hughton. My own assumption was that Newcastle would review immediately which players were 'bankers' (to be retained at almost any cost) and that a substantial incentive bonus would be paid to selected players, based upon the league position achieved at the end of the season. Their current package would be similarly reviewed with Hughton and adjusted where any serious imbalance existed.

Thirdly, that when priority acquisitions were agreed, a watch would be kept on any of these players who seemed to be 'open to a change of club' and some flexibility of timing would be possible. I assumed that Ashley, Lambias and Hughton would complete all the discussions necessary in the close season to ensure that the club was focussed on consolidating their recently regained Premiership status.

I was in exactly the same position as most of you in that I had no inside knowledge of what discussions were held or what decisions were made or by whom. However, I really believed that Ashley and his inner cabinet would reach a view similar to mine. In shorthand this would be as follows.

1. Retain (Bankers) Harper, Enrique, Coloccini, Barton, Nolan, Carroll and Gutierrez. Many other squad members were useful contributors but these seven were crucial. Barton, Nolan and Carroll also had serious question marks due to their erratic disciplinary and/or fitness record for which reliable cover/ substitutes must be provided.

2. I felt comfortable with the publicly stated 'wait-and-see policy' in relation to player acquisitions provided that early results did not call for more immediate action and felt that greater confidence in the manager and the experience of three years' ownership would guarantee that happened. The minimum priorities were likely to be two additional strikers followed by another central defender and a holding midfielder, all of Premiership quality.

3. My one serious doubt was the continuance of an unchanged hierarchy with wafer thin knowledge of the game despite the fact that Ashley had publicly confessed his shortcomings in his apology for previous errors. On the one hand can a leopard change its spots, on the other he had a valuable investment to protect or grow and unless he did correct this deficiency, how could he achieve that objective?

4. On balance I was hopeful, bearing in mind that the two clubs promoted with Newcastle were unlikely to stay in the Premiership for long and there were at least seven others whose long term membership of the Premiership was in serious doubt.

So much for logic, theory and assumption! What happened and why it happened is much more important and relevant. As events unfolded some clear flaws in my assumptions began to emerge but not for some time.

Having experienced what actually happened in the 2010/11 season as described in Chapter 15 I was pre-occupied with what, if anything, was being done at St James' to remedy the absence of a clear strategy for success at a Premiership Football Club. That there was such a need was, in my view, beyond reasonable doubt!

In June 2011, my own scorecard, based on matching what I believe should have happened against what had actually happened read as follows:

1. A stable management team, empowered to manage – FAILED
2. An agreed plan to strengthen the first team squad – FAILED
3. An agreed need to build a strike force capable of scoring 60+ goals per season – FAILED
4. A clear strategy to correct the errors exposed in the 2010/11 season – UNKNOWN

Why had Hughton been sacked, early attempts to strengthen the squad abandoned, the leading goal scorer sold without a replacement and with little comment from the club about future intentions?

The need to score the 60+ goals in the Premiership has been underscored over many seasons and only the top 4 achieved that target and reached 60+ points in 2010/11. Interestingly Newcastle's tally of 41 goals in home games was second only to Manchester United's as Champions whereas Newcastle's away goals total was the joint lowest in the Premiership. I concluded that whatever has been said, the crippling handicap at St James' was that no one with the power to change matters also had the required knowledge to inform their actions.

Reflecting on this, I had reached the conclusion that it was a strategy by default. It was one of survival if possible whilst spending the minimum and hoping for a 12th place or better. So, forget strategic thinking or targeted investment. I have searched and failed to find a better explanation for the bizarre events of December 2010 and January 2011.

Yet I can see what might have actually happened and why. Whether right or wrong, it seems to fit the facts.

> Carroll was plaguing Hughton with demands for a substantial pay hike. Hughton, being aware of Carroll's value to the squad and the absence of anyone other than Nolan to contribute the goals necessary to survive or prosper, ultimately pleaded for some concession. He was faced with the counter-argument that Carroll's behaviour both on and off the field did not justify the cost which meant that if he persisted, he would be sold. Hughton argued that was not his understanding of previous agreements. Pardew was approached told the conditions of accepting, agreed and Chris Hughton was then sacked. There is no evidence in Alan Pardew's previous record of outstanding success to which any managerial change could be attributed. Nor did Chris Hughton's own record justify such drastic action. Almost certainly after Carroll's goals and his England cap, some agents would have been checking his 'availability'.

To end where I started, are you surprised that it was the Sepp Blatter affair which triggered this train of thought? 'Newcastle United in crisis? What crisis?'

And I was still looking forward to the kick off of the 2011/2012 season ... but girding my loins for a rough ride! Perhaps someone at St James' might just read the book and wonder ... what if?

(First published as an article in *The Mag*
the Newcastle fanzine in June 2011)

18

Financial Prudence,
Disposal or Ambition?

Before the 2011/12 season kicked off on 13 August there was a flurry of activity by Newcastle in the transfer market with Kevin Nolan leaving in June to rejoin his old boss Sam Allardyce, the resident Manager when Mike Ashley acquired control of United, at West Ham for a fee said to be £3.5 million. There were eleven players released, including Sol Campbell, for whom no fees were sought or paid. Perhaps reduction of the payroll was the justification? Finally, Enrique left to join his former colleague Andy Carroll at Liverpool, without the fee being disclosed. Given his performances in United's colours that surely would have been a substantial sum?

However, there were some intriguing signings in the same June–August window, since they included three French players and an Italian – Cabaye, Marveaux, Obertan and Santon – for whom undisclosed fees were paid. United also signed a Senegalese international, Demba Ba, from West Ham, for whom no transfer fee was paid. West Ham had signed him from a German club on a contract which enabled Ba to leave without hindrance if West Ham were relegated from the Premiership, they were, he left and Newcastle benefitted. Perhaps pursuit of financial prudence was just a coincidence of a strategy shared by the two owners? What was certain was that we had now lost both the leading scorers of the last 2 seasons and, in return, we now had some untried midfield players plus a striker on a free transfer, to replace them. My concerns of last season remained, that United's ability to score the number of goals required to move up the table to consolidate their regained Premiership status, was in serious doubt.

After an intensive warm-up programme of 6 games, 3 of which were in the USA, those doubts remained undiminished as the strike force comprised the two Ameobi brothers, Best, Lovenkrands and the newcomer Ba. With the first game at home to Arsenal, who had never finished lower than 4th in Wenger's fifteen years as Manager, this was going to be a very good test.

So the season kicked off on Saturday 13 August before a crowd of 47,000 and finished, as it started, 0-0. A draw against Arsenal was okay but without a goal and with Ba, one of three debutants, substituted after half-time it was disappointing. Barton played and was lucky not to be sent-off, and afterwards indulged in his customary clumsy 'tweeting', a clear sign he wouldn't be at St James' much longer. A week later United won away to Sunderland, 1-0, with a set piece goal by Ryan Taylor while Ba sat the game out on the substitutes' bench and Barton received his second successive yellow card! A mid-week Carling cup tie away to Scunthorpe followed, was won after extra time, before Fulham were the visitors to St James' with United winning 2-1. Leon Best scored both goals and Ba appeared as a sub for Lovenkrands after an hour. Barton wasn't in the starting line up, United were 6th with 7 points after 3 games but having scored only 3 goals! By Monday 12 September when they travelled to London to play QPR, Barton had been given a free transfer to join QPR and turned out for the opposition before a meagre crowd of 16,000 fans for another 0-0 draw. That was enough to move an unbeaten United up to 4th despite the scarcity of goals. My concerns and no doubt those of many others grew despite their 4th position, an unbeaten record and only 1 goal conceded in the 4 games. Newcastle next travelled to Birmingham for the match away to Aston Villa which ended, yet again, in a draw, 1-1 with Best the United goal scorer and Ba being substituted. Hardly inspiring but with United still hanging on to 4th place and with a miserly defence refusing to 'leak' goals, a good team spirit was emerging with Stephen Taylor and Coloccini at the core. But when was the lack of goals scored going to be addressed? The answer was to come surprisingly quickly, in fact one week later when they were to entertain Blackburn Rovers at St James' after another hard earned mid-week Carling Cup win away to Nottingham Forest. Against Blackburn another 46,000 crowd witnessed an exciting display of goal scoring by Ba who scored a hat-trick within a thirty-minute spell before he was substituted in the second half with the game won 3-1. Dared we hope that this really was the turning point? One week later United travelled back to the Midlands again, this time to face Wolverhampton Wanderers and coming away with another victory, 2-1, buoyed by another Ba goal. These matches were followed by a 2-2 draw at home against Spurs with Ba scoring to equalise a Van de Vaart penalty and Shola Ameobi levelling the scores after Defoe had put Spurs in front for a second time; a 1-0 home win against Wigan in which

Cabaye scored to underline his value and increasing influence; a 3-1 away win at Stoke when Ba once more scored all 3 goals and a 2-1 win at home against Everton before the season's best attendance of 51,000!

It was time to draw breath after 11 games in which Newcastle were unbeaten and looking justifiably secure in 3rd position. Why all the doubts about Ashley, Pardew and the loss of the four most influential members of the successful Championship winning squad? On 5 November prior to a two-week fixture break because of International matches, the statistics were: P 11 W 7 D 4 L 0 and they were one of only two unbeaten Premiership sides. I, like most other fans was both delighted and surprised but I still questioned what Ashley's objectives and strategy really were? Was he going to build on success or feel 'job done'! However, it was a case of just enjoy it while it lasts. Yet United were over dependent on Ba with support from Best to score goals and on the defensive trio partnership of Steven Taylor, Coloccini and goalkeeper Krul to deny the opposition goals. My worries about the lack of reserves remained and the injury list was growing.

The next 2 games were both in Manchester to face on successive Saturdays, the top two sides in the Premiership. Manchester City were top with a 5-point advantage over their neighbours, unbeaten and having scored 39 goals with the second-best defensive record of 10 conceded and a GD of +29 against Newcastle's +9 while Manchester United had scored 28 times with a GD of +16, but were only 1 point better off than Newcastle. Toon fan's expectations were inflated to an unrealistic level and Newcastle came away with only a single point from the 6 on offer. True, they lost to City 1-3 having conceded 2 penalties with a not yet fully fit Ben Arfa and Sammy Ameobi supporting Ba, an attack always unlikely to produce a better result. At Old Trafford against Manchester United Newcastle drew 1-1 with Ba scoring the equalising goal from the penalty spot in the second half. Thus they left Manchester having lost their unbeaten record and with their forward line's frailties exposed, preparing to face Chelsea, then only 1 point behind Newcastle, at St James' one week later. Not only Chelsea was close behind them now in the Premiership table, so too were Arsenal and Liverpool, both on 23 points. This game, the anniversary of Pardew taking over from Hughton, saw the rock solid Newcastle defence with the best record in the division take the field accompanied by an attack of Ba and Lovenkrands with support from Ben Arfa. The biggest attendance since 2008 ensured a lively reception for both teams with a derisive chant aimed at Mike Ashley because of his decision to rebrand St James' Park, The Sports Direct Arena. Newcastle lost Coloccini before a goal had been scored and by half time Ben Arfa had been replaced by Shola Ameobi with the score 0-1. United went on to lose through further late goals, in the 89th and 92nd minutes, to lose their unbeaten home record, almost inevitably as they failed to score for only the 3rd time in 14 matches. As a final blow both Chelsea and Arsenal 'leap-frogged' them in the Premiership table, pushing United to 6th. If the players, management or fans were looking for an easy return to winning ways away at Norwich for the second game in a six-match December programme, they were mistaken. Neither Steven Taylor nor Coloccini were fit to play while with Shola Ameobi starting as Ba's strike partner goals were unlikely to flow. United did well to hold the score to 1-1 at half time through a late goal by Ba just before the interval and despite another Ba goal, Norwich were the 4-2 winners. United slipped to 7th and returned to St James' to host newly promoted Swansea on the 17th. Although Coloccini and Tiote returned after injury and Best, the top scorer before Ba's appearance, started, the side had a patchwork look about it and a final score of 0-0 seemed almost inevitable. Newcastle went on to lose 2-3 at home to West Brom in the next game, the visitors' 3rd successive 3-goal tally against United in a game that seemed to follow a predictable path of Ba scoring twice to equalise West Brom's goals only for the visitors to score again in the 85th minute. However, Newcastle then travelled to Bolton and came away comfortable 2-0 winners with goals from Ben Arfa a few minutes after he replaced Best on the hour and the expected, as it seemed, goal by Ba for a welcome 3 points before playing and losing 1-3 away to Liverpool on 30 December, their last game of 2011.

It was a good time to take stock with the transfer window about to open, the finances in good shape and good progress made by a squad which had benefitted from the new signings, Coloccini's captaincy, a better team spirit and above all Ba's contribution as the leading goal scorer. The need remained for another top quality goal scorer and more quality reserves to understudy Coloccini and Taylor whose unbroken partnership at the heart of the defence had been primarily responsible for the 14-game undefeated spell.

Newcastle began the New Year in style with an excellent 3-0 home victory over Manchester United and Ba contributed another goal before departing for the Africa Nations Cup. After a break for an FA Cup 3rd Round tie, which they won, United defeated QPR 1-0 at home, were surprisingly beaten 0-1 in the FA Cup 4th round tie by Brighton, then hammered 2-5 at Fulham a week later but bounced back with 2 wins in five days, away to Blackburn 2-0 to go 5th followed by a 2-1 victory at St James' over Aston Villa. It had been a physically punishing spell of 7 games in four weeks, but it was the last of those games which had most significance because it marked the return of Ba from international duty as did his new partner up front Cisse, who had been signed from the German club FC Freiburg for an undisclosed fee. Both strikers had played for Senegal, and it was Cisse's debut made after 15 minutes when he replaced the injured Ryan Taylor. Alan Pardew's post match comment that *'they (Cisse and Ba) are a dangerous pair'* was followed by the comment *'We have dangerous strikers all over the place here because Shola and Besty have done well, Lovenkrands is there as well and Ben Arfa.'* Was this just manager-speak or was he really so naive? After comments like that it might have been expected that when they travelled to Tottenham a week later it was to suffer their heaviest defeat of the season 0-5 despite fielding both Ba and Cisse, the latter substituted after the 5th goal. They fell to 6th and held on to that despite a further 3 games without a win. At home to Wolves, United again had Ba and Cisse in the starting line up were 2-0 up at half time yet the visitors, who had sacked their manager Mick McCarthy midweek, scored twice in the second half for 2-2 draw. Cisse had scored Newcastle's first after only 6 minutes but was replaced by Ben Arfa when the scores had been levelled. At home again the following week the local derby with Sunderland produced a similar disappointment. Despite Ba and Cisse starting, Sunderland were 1-0 up at the interval, Cisse was replaced after 72 minutes by Shola Ameobi who scored in injury time to earn a draw. For the second successive week a 52,000 crowd had witnessed 2 similar disappointing matches even though United's chosen team was close to full strength. On next to the Emirates Stadium to face an Arsenal side which had made steady progress up the table since their goalless start to the season at St James' on the opening day. In an encouraging opening Ben Arfa scored to take the lead, Van Persie equalised but a dour defensive performance by United was squandered in the 95th and last minute when Arsenal scored to win 2-1.

As with every Newcastle team I have watched over the years such a run of indifferent form and results is in the genes. But this one caused doubts to arise which were specific to this team. Why had United scored only four times in the last 4 games or Ba, until then a prolific goal scorer, failed to score at all and Cisse scored only once? Had Cisse's assumption of the prized number 9 shirt caused a rift between these two? When would the team return to winning ways and consolidate their 6th place or better in the season's remaining games? Just as typically they answered some of those questions by peeling off a sequence of 6 successive victories between 18 March and 21 April to move up to 4th!

They beat Norwich 1-0, West Brom 3-1, Liverpool 2-0, Swansea 2-0, Bolton 2-0 and Stoke 3-0. This was Premiership-winning form. A maximum 18 points with 13 goals scored and only 1 conceded. Cisse had scored in all 6 matches and in 3 of those he had scored twice, a total of 9, the improving Ben Arfa had scored in 2 games and Cabaye, now increasingly influential had scored twice in the 3-0 win over Stoke. But, there is always a 'but', what had happened to Ba's goal scoring form? However, with only 4 games left to play, two of which would be very difficult, was it reasonable to harbour ambitions of a European Champions League place next season? Could United finish higher than 4th?

United travelled to Wigan for what seemed, on paper, to be the easiest of the last 4 games only to be demolished 4-0 by a rampant Wigan fighting impressively hard to preserve their Premiership status. The next game was only four days later away to Chelsea who had 'steamrollered' QPR 6-1 over the same weekend and were also preparing to face Liverpool in the FA Cup Final three days after they welcomed Newcastle to Stamford Bridge! They had also knocked the mighty Barcelona out of the European Champions League to reach the European Final in May after the conclusion of the Premiership season. Some task or some incentive – which was it to be for Newcastle United? United shrugged off the Wigan setback and before the usual partisan crowd at Stamford Bridge convincingly did what Barcelona had failed to do, beat Chelsea 2-0 with Cisse, continuing his own remarkable goal scoring form by scoring twice. They both bore the hallmark of a quality striker but his second, in the last minute of added time, had everyone present shaking their heads in disbelief that it had actually happened. It will probably be seen later as the goal of the season. It was Cisse's 13th goal, scored in 12 games and 11 starts. Newcastle were 5th and 3 points better off than Chelsea, behind them in 6th. However the enigma remained about Ba's loss of his goal scoring touch. After his own prolific run earlier in the season he had scored in his first game after returning from the Africa Nations Cup competition in which Cisse had also scored wearing the number 9 shirt on his debut. That had been 12 games ago and the need for an answer was becoming more urgent! Four days later United faced Manchester City at an exuberantly full St James' Park. That Newcastle had performed better this season than anyone had dared to hope was beyond argument but as ever expectations of a victory in this game against the most prolific goal scorers of the season, Premiership Champions designate in most people's eyes, and the team which had ended Newcastle's unbeaten run, were driven more by hope than reality. However with the score still 0-0 at half time, it was still possible. In the end Manchester won by 2-0 after making their full quota of substitutions. The game was effectively determined by two factors, the relative strength of Manchester's reserves against the much weaker Newcastle reserves and the lack of a goal from Ba, Cisse or anyone else in the black and white stripes. Of course there can always be upsets and unexpected results as had happened in their last game against Chelsea but this was always unlikely to be one of them. Manchester City's seasonal record of 90 goals with 38 of those being in away games was superior to Newcastle's 55 of which 21 were at home. Now a place in the Champions League next season might have gone but participation in the Europa League signalled a marked upswing in United's fortunes. All that was needed now was a convincing victory in the last game away to Everton in 7th place and a goal from Ba. Meanwhile Chelsea had gone on to beat Liverpool 2-1 at Wembley in the FA Cup Final causing great joy and a strengthened self-belief at Everton who were also certain to finish above their Merseyside rivals in the Premiership for the first time since 2004/05 season. Perhaps it was Everton's determination to finish ahead of Liverpool that won the day for them for Newcastle's display was feeble. United lost 1-3, with their only goal an 'own goal' scored by the Everton defender, Hibbert. Newcastle had lost three of their last 4 games scoring in only one, with Cisse their only goal scorer. All other five teams in the top 6 had won on the final day. Sadly this was the Newcastle performance we hoped had been banished from their repertoire.

Yes, it was real progress to finish 5th but they still could not score the 60-goal minimum to justify being there. They still had only scored 56 goals in total exactly as they had done last season in finishing 12th and still had a miniscule positive 'Goal Difference'. Manchester City had won the Premiership with 93 goals and had still only clinched it on a better 'Goal Difference' than Manchester United. In 1 of every 2 games, on average, throughout the season Newcastle scored only 1 goal (11 times) or didn't score at all (7 times) and never scored more than 3 goals in any league game. Having kept a tight rein on opposing sides for the first 12 league games their final 'Goals Against' record of 51 was poor.

For me, the key message is that until a team has strength in depth and can score more than 60 goals in a season, no team can expect to command a place in the top 6 of this league. The more important question, however, is how does Mr Ashley read this evidence? Much to occupy all of us and him in the few weeks before another season kicks off in mid-August.

19

What Next? A Review
of 2010–12 Seasons

The celebrations to mark Newcastle's overdue return to Premiership prominence will continue throughout the summer months of the close season until the whistle blows in August to start another long journey of Premiership action spanning ten months. This season, 2011/12, has brought a glimpse of the success that generations of Geordies had grown up believing would always be theirs. Yet this season has also generated similar expectations for Everton fans on Merseyside and Manchester City's supporters because both have outperformed their neighbours, Liverpool and Manchester United respectively. For some clubs, notably Bolton and Wigan, it has been the opposite, another season of constant struggle and worry. How we fans judge our team's performance depends to a large extent on what our real expectations were at the outset. Were they driven by hope or past results or management's declared ambitions or the owner's whims?

Every Newcastle fan will have rejoiced in their final placing and unlike the last eight years will have enjoyed more pleasure than pain. But more than that the emergence of Krul as a top-quality goalkeeper with years of potential ahead; of Coloccini as a leader and all round footballer of great skill; of the development in Gutierrez's positional flexibility to match his undoubted ball skills; the impact and potential of the new signings, Santon, Tiote, Cabaye, Ben Arfa, Ba and Cisse mark a great stride forward. While all of these players are either of Premiership quality or potential they number only nine and all will not always be available, as exemplified by Steven Taylor, the only other player on the books who qualifies to take the total to ten. As we know if we can field all ten we are a match for most but that's not good enough.

The evidence of the past 5 seasons in Mike Ashley's ownership makes it difficult to judge whether he wants to keep the club or sell it. We know he is an experienced businessman and thus in developing Sports Direct – the sports goods retailer not the Arena – he will have had to gauge when to invest with the objective of gain and when not to invest. How with all that experience could he publish a 'Mission Statement' for Newcastle United FC which stated '... the board is fully committed to achieving that success' and 'our aim is for a top ten finish ... in the Premier League', but otherwise full of the virtues of so called financial prudence. It may be relevant that the statement was published on 17 October after United had drawn 2-2 with Spurs at St James', were 3rd and unbeaten after 8 games and Ba signed on a 'free' had scored for the third successive match. Timing is everything!

We have had a wonderful season and some very talented players have been acquired but tell me, Mr Ashley or Mr Lambias, what really is your objective? My own experience as a businessman is that no business I have ever known has operated without a strategy from which financial and other plans are derived. Strategy often has to be modified to recognise a financial constraint but that is not how your Mission Statement reads. Nor are the actions in selling Carroll, Enrique and Nolan and releasing Barton before any replacements had been recruited consistent with pursuit of success. Of course everyone in the club from Alan Pardew upwards publicly emphasised the strength in depth of the squad referring to the Ameobi brothers, Best, Lovenkrands and occasionally naming others. As John McEnroe would have screamed, 'you cannot be serious'. To go undefeated for 12 games is an achievement that no-one should belittle and at least it took the highest scoring side in the league, Manchester City, to end it in November. Surely the lesson learned from that should have been that Newcastle should remedy the deficiencies in the squad particularly as it will become more attractive to aspiring young players to join Newcastle than it has been since the managerial reigns of Kevin Keegan in the '90s or Bobby Robson a decade ago? Now is the time to invest as well as, but in addition to, nurturing the talent we have.

No one business determines the going market rate for players in terms of transfer fees, salaries or bonuses. Of course, it is no more than good business practise to determine what you are prepared to pay and to set your range and limits to match the clubs perceived business needs and potential. That is no different to any other business, including Sports Direct or Newcastle United, except in the scale of what is demanded and the publicity any decisions attract. The most valuable asset in any Premiership football club is a quality striker with a proven goal scoring record. If you are unsure about this do read Chapter 21 and if necessary read it a second time! Most of the top ten Premiership clubs demonstrate by their actions that they fully understand this cardinal principle. To return to reality from theory, I do wonder, often worry, what the Board's response would be if a substantial offer is tabled for Cisse? Similarly, what the response would be if an increase in salary is sought by any of the key ten players I have listed? But why was I wondering when I read, literally as I wrote this, that in an interview with BBC Radio Newcastle Alan Pardew's response was, 'It's impossible to restrict Real Madrid, Barcelona, Chelsea, Manchester City coming in for one of our players. We have players who are not on the salaries these top clubs can offer. The one security I have is that Mike Ashley is a difficult seller. He is not going to let someone go for £7 million, he is going to want top, top money.' So there we all have it from the horse's mouth or, if you prefer, the Premier League manager of the season. Forget pledges to commit fully to the success of Newcastle United, forget pledges to respect fans and the local culture, forget team building for the affordable future. They have gone, along with the name 'St James' Park', all in the name of Financial Prudence@Sports Direct.com!

In summary, United made excellent progress last season and their top 6 finish is both an achievement and a rightful expectation just as much as it is for Arsenal, Chelsea, Manchester United, Tottenham and Liverpool and all except Liverpool achieved it. A top 6 finish should be seen as the standard for United every year and to finish lower than 6th but higher than 12th as unsatisfactory. More importantly with sensible policies, targeted investment and good management it should be easier to achieve that target than to fail.

How much better for the club's future prospects it would have been if a positive statement had been made which emphasised a policy of continuous, selective recruitment and further development of the existing squad rather than point to the owner's bargaining skills.

What next? Better to sell Newcastle United now to someone who will respect and nurture it, than to run it back into the ground by selling off the assets which promised so much. Alan Pardew's interview was the most blatant 'FOR SALE' sign that I have seen, timed on the eve of the final day of the season just as the June transfer window is about to open. 'Roll up! Roll up! Great bargains inside and the turnstiles open at 9 a.m. No reasonable offers refused!' I can't wait for the next Mission Statement.

20

Why the Golden Promise Was Never Fulfilled

Now that I have completed the story, which I hope has rekindled some memories, it is possible for all of us to take a balanced retrospective view of the twenty-year period since John Hall signed and published the Magpie Group document 'A Pledge for the Future', and began the process which led to his appointment to the Board, his Chairmanship, and finally his outright ownership of Newcastle United. It is important to remember that by the time the Hall and Shepherd families sold their shareholding to Mike Ashley, the pledges made in the original manifesto had long been abandoned by those who made them, and probably forgotten by most fans.

How it happened is part of the story I have recounted in preceding pages, and why it happened is what I now want to address. My reason for doing so is that a successful future for Newcastle United is dependent upon satisfactorily answering that question: 'Why?' The future will be very bleak indeed if the serious failings of this period are repeated. Sadly, Mike Ashley, who has now owned the club for 3 full seasons (the second of which was the last of Newcastle's first spell in the Premiership) has, however unintentionally, followed the same downward path which Newcastle United were on when he acquired the club. If anything, their last year in the Premiership, season 2008/09, was arguably the worst since the early 1980s and saw more managers dismissed and a deeper mistrust between the club and its supporters than at any other time in the club's 120-year history.

However, under his apparently reluctant ownership, the club has gone on to regain its lost Premiership status immediately and the fans should, indeed *must*, recognise that Mike Ashley can take some credit for that.

Thus, on a more encouraging note, I believe that even after this catastrophic period, the future for Newcastle could be extremely bright.

It is not that they are guaranteed a place in the top 6, or even a place in the Premiership, but I will attempt to demonstrate why I believe that should be the case, and how it can be achieved.

But before I attempt to do that, I must offer my own view as to why the mistakes made by both owners since 1990 occurred.

By the early 1980s, top-level professional football in the UK was under immense pressure to change, driven by a combination of economic and social factors nationwide. In that sense, professional football was no different to any other business – be it manufacturing, retailing, or any service industry in the UK. Most businesses, however, had already considered the need to take account of the changing context of everyday life when compiling their own future business plans, and had sound strategic principles to achieve these. While 'no strategy survives contact with reality', it is equally true that without some serious attempt to construct a model, significant errors are inevitable, with substantial financial pain as a result.

At that time, football clubs, whatever their level, tended to be run by a board of local establishment figures, often relatively wealthy men in professional occupations. Since their income was derived from their professional or business occupations, they sought no salary, nor were they paid any. None of the football clubs were publicly listed companies and no dividends were demanded or paid. It was a classic example of the British amateur doing something he loved, and whatever funds were required for the modest developments that were planned, the Board would subscribe collectively. Their reward was in engaging and participating in a game they loved by attending matches both at home and away in the best seats available with hotel accommodation provided as part of the club's travel plans. Players' wages, which had been limited by the Football League in conformity with the industrial practice of the time, had until recently been low and immutable. But now they were rising. These costs, together with those of maintaining the ground, were met from gate receipts. No other match day income, except for minimal match programme sales, was even contemplated in those days. There was neither demand nor facilities for catering, and no club shop.

Apparently unmoved by the changing context of everyday life, the Boardroom of most major Football League clubs continued to operate as a replica of a Victorian gentleman's club, even if the club was playing at the highest level with a playing staff including several internationals.

Spectator facilities at most grounds were minimal – usually stepped terraces with only a modest acknowledgement of safety concerns through the provision of anti-crush barriers. Hygiene needs were addressed by providing simple, communal urinals for 'men only' use. This was an obvious perpetuation of the old work environment, a 'them and us' or a 'bosses and workers' society. The bosses ran the clubs and the working lads played or watched.

The regulatory bodies of the Football Association and the Football League reflected the same class composition and seeming unawareness of, or indifference to, social and economic change.

Television viewing had already become the most popular entertainment choice in the UK more than two decades earlier, and yet crucially the FA resisted repeated pleas to permit the televising of league matches live, because they feared its impact on the principal source of income, gate receipts. The FA continued to restrict TV coverage mainly to the BBC and only permitted edited highlights, except for a handful of matches such as the Cup Final and some internationals. In these matters, the FA and the Football League were at also least two decades behind the pace of the retailing responses to changing consumer tastes.

This was already an anachronism, and it was inevitable that it would have to change. But as so often happens, the catalysts were unexpectedly three major disasters, which allied to the popularity of television viewing, combined to ensure that change would happen swiftly.

Between 1985 and 1989, three serious disasters occurred at football matches, resulting in a combined death toll of almost 200 fans, all involving English clubs: at Valley Parade, Bradford, the Heysel Stadium, Belgium, and at Hillsborough, Sheffield.

Finally, the dam of resistance burst when public concern over increasing outbreaks of serious hooliganism in major football cities merged with an awareness of safety shortcomings to trigger a series of major enquiries driven by the Government. The most far-reaching of these was the enquiry conducted by Lord Taylor, the Lord Chief Justice, into questions of public safety at football grounds, which led rapidly to the enactment of legislation requiring every major football ground, defined as the top two divisions of the Football League, to become an all-seater stadium by May 1994. The century-long tradition of standing on the terraces was finally over.

In another one of those strange coincidences that have linked my life with the history of Newcastle United and football in general, Lord Taylor, a Geordie, was a contemporary of one of my brothers and his father had been our family GP in Newcastle. Soon afterwards, Lord Taylor and I met in London as ambassadors for the City of Newcastle.

The convergence of improvements in football stadia and an acknowledgement of the inadequacy of football ground facilities was followed rapidly by the recruitment of a new audience. That new audience was comprised of what long-term football fans describe disparagingly as the 'grey suits'. At first, it seemed they simply wanted to attend high-profile sporting events in comfort.

That helped to drive the provision of vastly improved catering facilities, which in turn led to increased sponsorship and the whole cycle began to revolve – to the benefit of more traditional supporters and owners alike. It was inevitable that the new, wealthier fans, many of whom were businessmen who had previously watched rugby as their first choice, as opposed to the urban working man's lifelong preference for football, wanted not only to view in comfortable seats but frequently in private boxes. Ultimately, this started a trend towards attracting new supporters, who might also be potential shareholders or owners, to the game for pleasure. Some began to see opportunities to make money and attract publicity, but also with a promise of tangible benefits for long-term fans.

What I have described was a snapshot of the changing football scene nationally. Newcastle United and its home ground since its founding in 1892, St James' Park, fits the description precisely. More specifically, it was also the remorse over the lost glitz of Kevin Keegan's two years as a player in the mid-1980s which fuelled the desire of a number of businessmen on Tyneside to seek Board membership. At the time, there was an impassable barrier; the Board was, effectively, a closed shop, not allowing any sale or transfer of the limited number of shares in issue without the approval of all other Board members.

It was then that John Hall, having created MetroCentre, became attracted to the idea of gaining Board membership. Shrewdly, he could see that the easiest, perhaps the only way, to achieve that ambition was to enter into an alliance with an existing group – the self-styled Magpie Group, comprised of the vocal Newcastle Supporters' Association and some individual businessmen, who had been trying unsuccessfully for some time to break into Newcastle United's Boardroom to enforce what they believed to be much-needed change.

John Hall's increasing prominence and influence, his regular media appearances, and his financial clout made him an attractive recruit for the Magpie Group, and he became their leader and spokesman. They published their charter in 1988, signed by John Hall. His cash was used effectively to gain wider public support for change and to encourage shareholding Board members to sell out. It was an inducement most could not resist. The really curious thing is that until that time, John Hall had not been a regular football supporter, and if he had any affiliation, he admitted it was to Sunderland.

So the answer to my first question, 'Why were the published pledges of the Magpie Group Charter never fulfilled?' probably lies in what caused

John Hall's 'Damascene conversion', and in consequence him to attack the Newcastle Board by spending significant sums to oust the directors and acquire control.

The evidence is that on the back of MetroCentre's success and with a rampant Conservative Government led by Mrs Thatcher in her pomp, he had attracted the Prime Minister's attention by being a businessman/ entrepreneur in the preferred mould of that decade. He did this very successfully, though not without a hiccup or two along the way, by spotting a temptingly soft target in Newcastle United, setting his sights on it, and seizing it. Nothing on Tyneside has a higher public profile than Newcastle United Football Club, and it was now his to do with as he pleased.

By the time he had acquired all of the shares in Newcastle United with a token presence from some of his allies *en route*, he had become Sir John Hall. He had the nous to recruit a professional commercial director already experienced in football matters at Glasgow Rangers, Freddie Fletcher, and through Freddie the club began to develop the income-generating activities already established in more entrepreneurial clubs. More importantly, however, as the club was struggling in the Second Division (today's Championship), he looked for a Manager through whom he could develop the club. The evidence points to his accepting the recommendation of Fletcher that the one man who could do that was Kevin Keegan, the playing hero of a few years earlier.

Kevin was recruited and the Golden Promise appeared to be within reach. Indeed, the promise was repeated over and over again, each time becoming grander.

These were the early days of John Hall's frequent public statements about 'Geordieland' – a separate nation of 'Geordie people' within the UK. His public intention was to create a Newcastle Sporting Club, embracing rugby, basketball, ice hockey, and other sporting facilities, for everyone on Tyneside. It would rival best European practice by becoming a 'Barcelona upon Tyne'. The fans bought into this dream readily; the evidence of match days testified to its reality. Yet even as John Hall's propaganda machine was in full flow, there was an even bigger struggle going on in the corridors of power at the Football Association Headquarters.

It had rumbled on from the mid-1980s to the end of 1990 before it crystallised in a challenge by a group of major successful First Division clubs declaring their intention to break away from the Football League to create an autonomous Premiership if the FA continued to oppose the concept. They were serious. The driver of this of course was the lure of money, much more money than ever before. Commercial television and satellite TV companies in particular had already decided that they had a better developed strategy to exploit successfully the growing appeal of football, which was for them to televise live top-level football in the UK, for which they were prepared to pay mouth-watering sums of money. The initial Premiership membership was comprised of clubs who had bought into this strategy, and they designed the Premier League for their own purposes!

This is also important in the context of 'How to succeed', which I will deal with in the next chapter. But I still want to stay focused on the reasons why Newcastle failed, and the lure of riches is an important element. The need to get into the Premiership because of its burgeoning financial attractiveness meant that John Hall was prepared to invest heavily to do so, and with the success of his MetroCentre development and its later sale in 1995, he was financially in a position to do so.

However, it also caused John Hall to shorten his horizons much more towards short-term success rather than a more credible medium-term achievement of his objectives. It was one thing to be necessarily short-term to achieve promotion to the Premiership, which was the challenge he had faced in spring '92 when Newcastle had narrowly avoided relegation to the former Third Division, but it was another thing to maintain the same short-term focus once they were in the Premiership. The following season (1992/93) they went on to win promotion as league Champions and they were in the Premiership for only its second full season of 1993/94. Unhelpfully, the financial pressure of guaranteeing additional investment, while Sir John simultaneously provided for the needs of his principal property development business, was becoming more onerous, if still sustainable.

Newcastle United achieved more than could have been reasonably expected with a sequence of outcomes which were precocious for new entrants to the Premiership. They finished 3rd, 6th, 2nd, and 2nd in successive years. For John Hall, this instant success changed everything, and if the future he planned was no longer based on the Magpie Group's concept of democratisation, it was still attractive to fans as he eulogised about winning the Premiership, getting into the Champions League, winning the Champions League and, along the way, winning the FA Cup. The roots of future crippling problems should have been obvious to all of us during this period.

The first problem was that there was no objective, external, experienced voice to offer an alternative view at board level. John Hall, the visionary and founder of Cameron Hall Developments, his son Douglas, his Managing Director Russell Jones, and Freddy Shepherd, a businessman ally, constituted the Newcastle United Board.

During my time on the Board, I became aware that many of them were used to taking major decisions in the same unstructured 'off the cuff' way. This would have been a high-risk strategy at any time, but in the complex, fast-changing world of an as-yet-unformed Premiership, it was never going to be adequate. But it was their way of running a private business. It was almost as if they believed that simply by insisting that Newcastle *must* win something quickly, they would succeed. 'Where there is a will there is a way,' was the dictum, and it never seemed to occur to them collectively that they were imposing unsustainable pressure on Kevin Keegan.

But that is what happened, and it exposed the second major problem. Kevin Keegan eventually collapsed emotionally under the weight of demands and unrealistic expectations. Abruptly, he left the club. What triggered that was just one of the consequences of seeking a listing on the London Stock Exchange, which was the Board's chosen route to funding the pursuit of success and, in doing so, crystallising their own wealth.

John Hall and Cameron Hall Developments had decided that they needed to tap into new sources of funds, and a public listing at a time when the stock market was buoyant, when football was a vogue sector, and the financial attraction of investment in the Premiership was widely recognised, seemed an obvious conclusion. It is not a step that any private company should take without very careful thought, because management styles seldom adapt easily to that required of a publicly quoted company. The Newcastle United Board's behaviour is a perfect case study of this. Nevertheless, the decision to seek a listing was taken and this caused an irreversible shift in the fortunes of both Newcastle United and the Hall family. As an experienced journalist was to suggest some years later, it seemed as if Newcastle United had been transformed from a promotional vehicle for supporting Sir John's ambition to achieve regional prominence, into a cash cow to provide financial sustenance for the family business, Cameron Hall Developments. To meet the listing requirements, Sir John was obliged to stand down from the Board and progressively thereafter he withdrew, making only random appearances while control passed nominally to Douglas, his son, and leadership of the Board to Freddy Shepherd, who became Chairman of both the club and the PLC in 1999.

Perversely, the scandal of 1998 ultimately gave Shepherd and the younger Hall a mechanism to remove the independent directors from the Board. Newcastle United was back to where it had been before 1990, except for the change of faces from the 'old guard', who had been professional men, working for the love of the game. The new Board initially had set an agenda for change adopted from John Hall's work with supporters' groups a decade earlier. The Magpie Group had highlighted the failings of the previous ruling autocracy as not responding to the need for change, a lack of investment, and a need for improved management. John came to power with a pledge of democratisation, promising to embrace fans' views, revitalise the Board, and invest to bring success on the field and better facilities off it.

The Board, from 1999, effectively went on to ignore the listing obligations and only satisfied the corporate governance code of best practice by invoking the clause to 'comply or explain'. While good corporate governance does not guarantee success, wanton abandonment of good practice *always* ends in disaster, which was indeed the fate that befell Newcastle United.

However, their salaries increased – unlike those of their unpaid predecessors – to a level that, when they quit, both Douglas Hall and Freddy Shepherd were being paid £500,000 per year, to reflect 'increased responsibilities', while the Hall and Shepherd families were collecting dividends in aggregate of £2.7 million per annum, authorised by themselves. The company was sold in 2007 when there was no cash left to pay a dividend in 2006. In that period, from flotation in 1997 to the sale in 2007, they had sold shares (including the final transaction with Mike Ashley) to realise almost £100 million, to which payments of dividends, salaries, and other benefits contributed another £52 million. Did their performance over that period justify such rewards?

In United's 11 seasons in the Premiership under their ownership, they employed 10 managers, of whom only two were successful, Kevin Keegan and Bobby Robson. They disillusioned Keegan and brutally sacked Robson. They never understood the Premiership, nor their managers, but they did increase their own personal wealth significantly.

Any success was short-lived, democratisation an illusion, and revitalisation of the Board was discarded. By the time the business was sold, it was in financial chaos. Financially, it was in a worse state in 2007 than it had been in 1990, when John Hall acquired it.

During their seventeen years of ownership, their ambitions appear to have changed diametrically from public cause in the interest of the city, the fans, and the North East as a whole, to be replaced by an apparent need 'to milk the cash cow'. Sadly, Keegan and Robson had both known how to achieve what the Board wanted and what the fans continued to want – sustainable success in the upper reaches of the Premiership. Given reassurance, understanding, and a proper support structure, they could have delivered that.

Keegan's strategy was intuitive, not formalised, but was admirable, timely, appropriate, and very successful, yet he resigned because he did not feel he could continue. Why? Because without support and under increasing pressure to 'win silverware now', he lost belief in himself. It was too late then to reclaim him with promises.

The Hall and Shepherd axis really believed that almost anyone they appointed could do what Keegan had done, and they demonstrated this fallacy by repeatedly appointing people who could not approach Keegan's success – except for Bobby Robson, who brought with him a knowledge that was critical to the Premiership from 2000 onwards, which was how to successfully handle foreign players, who for obvious reasons now dominate the squads of the top clubs.

I remain confident that the blueprint for success remains the same now as that which I presented to Freddy Shepherd when I was a Board member in 1997/98. The prediction I made at the time is underscored by the results in the Premiership since.

But read on and you can make up your own mind as to whether I am right or wrong in holding my view. If you are able to unearth a better reason for the death of the promise, so be it!

21

The Premiership,
and How to Succeed in It

Powered by satellite TV money and building on the precedent he had
set in the USA and Australia, Rupert Murdoch was determined to use
high-profile sports fixtures to increase his market share in the UK.
Inevitably, Murdoch's focus was on the top football clubs and the mass
following football had here. He sought to employ the same methods here
that he had adopted with such success elsewhere, but he was initially
baulked by the Football Association. They were resistant to the idea of
televising live league matches, particularly the Premier League, on the
grounds that to do so would have a serious, adverse affect on attendances
at all other football clubs. In addition, and as part of a more entrenched
attitude to UK broadcasting, they sought to continue their longstanding
arrangements with the BBC, who were happy to screen only the
occasional live match, usually the FA Cup Final and some international
games, accompanied by edited highlights of league games. The BBC was
also anxious to avoid any criticism of their use of licence fee money,
which in consequence would inhibit the corporation from bidding
for rights in an open competition for live match screening, even if
the FA relaxed its stance.

   However, it was the top football clubs, those most likely to benefit from
the large sums of money being dangled before them for the television
rights of live matches, who threw down the gauntlet. In a published
declaration of intent, they threatened to form a breakaway league
without sanction from the FA if the latter did not agree to the creation of
what is known now as the Premiership. They pushed the matter as far as
the ten clubs who led the charge could in 1991, when the reality of their
threat led swiftly to agreement and the Premiership began its life for the
season 1992/93 with the twenty-two clubs which otherwise would have

comprised the First Division. At that time, Newcastle United was on a charge in the new First Division, formerly of course the Second Division, and in a highly successful season, which they finished as Champions, they gained entry to the new Premiership in only its second season.

After an extremely successful start to life in the Premiership, the Board of Newcastle United embarked on a full London Stock Exchange listing in 1996/97 and as a result was obliged to recruit a minimum of three external directors, including one as Chairman, and I was one of those three. By then the attractiveness and value of the Premiership was confirmed for all parties – Sky Television, the Premiership clubs, the Football Association, and all football fans – who were uniformly delighted with the outcome. Sky, because the company had used it successfully as a battering ram to create substantial market share for all of its channels, the clubs, because Sky was ready to increase the value of their already considerable sponsorship, the FA, because televising live matches was having a beneficial impact on the level of interest in football nationally, and the fans, who could now watch additional matches at home. It was, after all, the principal national team sport in the UK, and this exposure simply increased its dominance.

By the time I had joined the Board of Newcastle United, the Premier League was completing its fifth season, in which Newcastle finished 2nd for the second year in succession. I, no doubt like many of you, had observed the changing character of the game since the birth of the Premiership and its impact on the complement of clubs which had formed it initially. I sought to create a model of those characteristics and to match them with the characteristics of clubs most likely to succeed by establishing and validating the inherent values of history, location, and a loyal fan base to football clubs. Had this provided, as I suspected it had, a platform for success? To this I added my own analysis of the best way to exploit these pre-existing conditions to guarantee success, provided that 'success' met my definition of consistently achieving a place in the top 6 of the Premiership every year. To do this I used my experience as a football fan since birth and my experience as a businessman, to which I could now also add a view from a Premiership Club Board. I called this simply, 'How to succeed in the Premiership – Cassidy's Law of Football'. In this I tried to take full account of the existing characteristics, which, while undeniably accidents of history, are real and therefore critical to a high probability of success, as I will explain. I describe them as preconditions.

The preconditions are for the club to have **a history of success, a stadium of an acceptable size and quality**, and, as a result of this, **an established attendance base** of circa 35,000 plus. In addition, these clubs must be located in **an area that can naturally attract local sponsorship** from the business community. Ideally, it will be **a geographically discrete television area**, to which we must add the variables of **a capacity to fund the initial investment** required and a readiness to **maintain investment** at an appropriate level.

To optimise these pre-existing conditions, the Board must ensure that it has a **Manager/Coach** who understands the changing demands of the Premiership, supported by **an appropriate football management structure** working within **clearly defined roles** to **a clear strategic plan established and funded by the Board**. Easy to stipulate, but difficult to implement, perhaps? I would argue not, and I will demonstrate this later.

Given what I have written about the development and history of the game, I accepted at that time, 1997/98 – and my view has not changed in the years since – that the heartland of football would provide most of the natural contenders and therefore my predicted list of potentially successful clubs was likely to be limited to those in major cities of the Midlands and North, the industrialised heartland of the UK. However, London also has to figure because of its pulling power as the capital. It, too, has its industrialised zones, and a long association with league football, but because London clubs are less geographically discrete, the selection of those clubs is slightly more difficult.

By my definition, the obvious contenders were clubs from Birmingham, Manchester, Liverpool, Newcastle, Sheffield/Leeds, and London. Those are the cities that match the criteria I specified, but by applying current stadium quality, size, fanbase, and history, the clubs I chose from those areas were refined to Liverpool, possibly challenged by Everton, Manchester United, possibly challenged by Manchester City, Newcastle United, and Aston Villa, possibly challenged by Birmingham City or West Bromwich Albion.

London has to include Arsenal, the club with the longest continuous presence of any club in the top division, having never been out of the top division since 1919/20. On the history criterion alone, I would have added Tottenham Hotspur. On the grounds of what was already beginning to happen at Chelsea, I ranked them close to, although behind, Spurs.

The quality of management at that time was unquestioned only at Manchester United. All others had experienced many changes in management and all were to experience changes in ownership, not only necessary to meet more stringent financial criteria but also because of growing recognition by outsiders of what were seen as the potential financial rewards of a well-run football business.

The strategic plan that the Board has to formulate should be based on my definition of success: the club should seek to achieve a top 6 place in the Premiership every year. As a footnote, it is revealing that many Arsenal fans were disenchanted in 2009 because Arsène Wenger had not won any 'silverware' in the season and had not topped the Premiership since the season 2003/04. Yet Wenger's record is second only to that of Sir Alex Ferguson and Manchester United. Arsenal have been in the top four of the Premier League continuously since he joined the club in 1996/97 – an improvement on the 10th, 4th, 12th, and 5th places in the preceding seasons. He has also worked remorselessly and successfully, not only to create teams playing attractive attacking football but also to spot and nurture young talent, of whom Thierry Henry and Cesc Fàbregas are only two examples. That constitutes success.

While the target finish is a top four position – because currently that bestows the additional benefit of automatic Champions League entry – I believe that should be enlarged to a focus on a top 6 spot. Derived from this, the management team should assemble a squad capable of achieving a minimum of 60 points in a 38-match season. The rationale for this is that no club has yet achieved a top four place with less than 60 points and in six of the fifteen years of a 20-team Premiership, 60 points only guaranteed a top 6 position. In 2 seasons – 1995/96 and 2009/10 – 60 points only achieved 8th position.

Managers cannot build a squad to achieve 60 points, but they can assemble one to score 60 goals or more per season, which was my suggestion in 1997. Perhaps that was heavily influenced by my long history as a Newcastle fan. Certainly, Kevin Keegan's player acquisitions and playing style reinforced my belief. However, it is borne out by results since. There have been only 5 seasons when teams scoring 60 or more goals were 7th or lower. In aggregate, only six clubs were involved.

Armed with that information, the club from the Boardroom downwards can plan and evaluate the costs and resources required.

In many respects, the results of the first 3 seasons of the Premiership should be discarded, simply because too many of the initial complement of clubs did not conform to the criteria I have established – history, stadium, fanbase, and discrete television area – and were therefore unlikely to survive as the Premier League took shape. You might find it surprising, but at least half of the clubs in that first season had, by my criteria, virtually no chance of remaining in the league. These teams included Norwich City (3rd in the first season), Queens Park Rangers (5th), Wimbledon (12th), Coventry, Ipswich, Southampton, Oldham, Crystal Palace, and Nottingham Forest. Six of those were relegated in the first 3 seasons, along with some equally unlikely clubs like Swindon and Leicester, who were promoted and relegated in the same three years.

What many clubs in the Premiership, or those in the Championship with aspirations to achieve promotion to it, appear not to have understood fully is that it has changed significantly in its 20 seasons to date, attracting considerably increased sponsorship and television revenues. These income streams have underpinned a similar pattern of increasing revenues to reward success in the UEFA Champions League.

Those changes resulted in an urgent need for better quality financial management to be added to a strengthened football management team because of the substantial cash flows which now arose. Consequently, those clubs which did not have adequate financial or managerial controls and who were already operating close to their maximum debt facility quickly found themselves facing a threatening insolvency problem.

This had been created because they were drawn by the lure of potential riches in the Premiership and most were badly burned by the cost of a predictable failure to achieve them. A combination of their inability to consider the probability of success or failure was, in no small measure, due to fans' own unmodified ambitions. In summary, no credible strategic plan existed, and in the worst cases, a plan was not thought to be necessary.

Now look back to my stipulated 'preconditions for success' set out earlier and compare that with the list of those who were in the Premiership when it was formed in 1992 or have achieved promotion to it since. Consider the results; is this a self-fulfilling prophecy, or a coincidence?

- **Burnley:** promoted '09, relegated '10
- **Wolverhampton:** promoted '03, relegated '04, promoted '09, relegated ?
- **Swindon Town:** promoted '94, relegated '95, *insolvency '00 and '02*
- **Watford:** twice promoted and relegated the following season, '00 and '07
- **Barnsley:** promoted and relegated after one season, '98, *insolvency '02*
- **Oldham Athletic:** inaugural 2 seasons, relegated '94, *insolvency '03*
- **Hull City:** *insolvency '01*, promoted '08, relegated '10
- **Bradford City:** promoted '99, relegated '00, *insolvency '02*
- **Crystal Palace:** inaugural '92, relegated '93, promoted '94, '97, '04, relegated '95, '98, '05, *insolvency '02*
- **West Bromwich:** never higher than 17th, promoted '02, '04, '08, '10, relegated '03, '06, '09
- **Stoke City:** promoted '08, relegated ?

- **Sheffield United:** inaugural 2 seasons, relegated '94, promoted '06, relegated '07
- **Reading:** promoted '06, relegated '08
- **Ipswich:** inaugural 3 seasons, relegated '95, promoted '00, relegated '02, *insolvency '03*
- **Norwich:** inaugural 3 seasons, relegated '95, promoted '04, relegated '05
- **Wigan:** promoted '05, relegated ?
- **Nottingham Forest:** inaugural season, relegated '93, promoted '94, '98, relegated '97, '99
- **Birmingham:** promoted '02, '07, '09, relegated '06, '08
- **Queens Park Rangers:** inaugural 4 seasons, relegated '96, *insolvency '01*
- **Derby County:** promoted '96, '07, relegated '02, '08
- **Portsmouth:** *insolvency '99*, promoted '03, relegated '10, *insolvency '10*
- **Coventry:** inaugural 9 seasons, relegated '01, never higher than 11th

Of the forty-three clubs which have played in the Premiership since its inaugural season, those are statistically the worst-performing 22. Therefore, the remaining 21 are better able to compete. However, the margin of difference between them, taking into account statistics and history, suggests that many of these clubs too are vulnerable. These are:

- **Leicester:** promoted in '94, '96, '03, relegated '95, '02, '04, *insolvency '02*, achieved 9th, 10th, 8th in successive seasons '96–'99
- **Charlton Athletic:** promoted '98, relegated '99, promoted '00, relegated '07, achieved 7th and 9th
- **Fulham:** promoted '01, now in 9th consecutive season, highest 7th in '09, played in final of Europa League in '10
- **Wimbledon:** inaugural season until relegated '00, *insolvency '03*, now Milton Keynes Dons, not a contender
- **Sheffield Wednesday:** inaugural season until relegated '00
- **Bolton Wanderers:** promoted in '95, '97, '01, relegated '96, '98, continuous place in Premiership since '01
- **Southampton:** inaugural members, relegated '05, *insolvency '09*
- **Leeds United:** inaugural members, in top 6 seven times and 3rd once, until relegated '04, *insolvency '04*
- **Blackburn Rovers:** marginal candidates for Premiership without hope of a sustainable top 6 position

In addition, Blackpool, promoted in '10, are unlikely to survive long.

This analysis validates my contention that only about 12 clubs are capable of meeting the required criteria currently for sustainable occupancy of a top 6 Premiership place.

At the upper end of the table, there have been fewer surprises since the Premier League took shape, particularly after its reduction in size, to a twenty-club league in 1995/96.

Only Leeds and Blackburn have made the top 6 more than once, while West Ham, Bolton, and Ipswich have achieved it only on one occasion. The latter three are no more than the expected random statistical occurrence and cannot be considered as serious contenders.

Blackburn demonstrate that a top-quality striker can provide the goals required, but sustainable success depends on funding, which may be limited. The three Sheffield/Leeds clubs should be able to provide a challenge at the top, but only Leeds, consistently in the top 6 until 2002, came close. It may be too costly after relegation and insolvency in 2003/04 to rebuild it now. Yet we should not regard that as impossible.

But it is the current 'Big Four' who prove my case: Manchester United, Arsenal, Chelsea, and Liverpool. Manchester United is literally in a league of its own at present, having won the title eleven times. The team has never been out of the top three. Arsenal is a good second, but only since Wenger's recruitment. He has won the title three times, has been runner-up five times, and has never been out of the top four. Chelsea ranks third – never in the top 6 until 1996/97 but never out of the top 6 since, improving from 2000 when they began to score 60+ goals every season. In the 6 seasons since Abramovitch acquired the club in June 2003, Chelsea has always won or been the runner-up, except for 2008/09 when the team finished 3rd. Abramovitch ensured this progression continued under a series of experienced foreign managers. Liverpool is fourth of four, and by most tests looks to be vulnerable. It has never won the Premiership, has only been runner-up once and has twice not even made the top 6. It has frequently fallen short of the 60-goals-per-season standard.

Its salvation has been the weakness of the contenders, and yet at present it faces the biggest local threat of 'neighbouring' contenders in Everton. In the last five years, Everton has finished 4th once, 5th three times, and 6th once. Aston Villa and Newcastle United are the greatest underperformers of those teams who should be camped in the top 6, neither having won the title. But Newcastle is ahead of Villa by virtue of twice being runner-up to Villa's once, and with two 3rd places against Villa's none.

Aston Villa, Liverpool, and Everton account for 16 of the 34 occasions that a team scoring less than 60 goals has achieved a top 6 place – Aston

Villa seven times, Liverpool five, and Everton four – which underlines the weakness of their competitive threat to Manchester United, who have only once failed to score 60 goals. Arsenal's team have failed twice, Chelsea three times, all more than ten years ago.

Newcastle does not have a contender in the same city, nor does it have a serious threat from its neighbours. Neither Middlesbrough nor Sunderland look capable of sustaining long-term superiority over it. Aston Villa should view their neighbouring candidates, West Bromwich Albion and Birmingham, as equally unlikely usurpers. However, in reality, the competition for the top 6 places is between all of the candidate clubs I have mentioned, probably twelve in total.

As always, there were a number of unforeseen consequences to the creation of the Premiership, prime among which was the need for English football clubs to attract more foreign players than before, effectively reversing the previous pattern of Continental European Clubs buying top Football League players.

This arose from the ongoing need to strengthen playing squads quickly with established top-flight players, which could not be met as in the past, by transfers from lower leagues in the UK. The appeal of buying international players was first demonstrated for me by Keegan's imaginative signings at Newcastle. While his principal strikers were British, the balance of his attacking sides was possible only by his intelligent sorties to European clubs.

This was helped both by his stature as a former player and his personal knowledge after his successful spell as a player in the German Bundesliga. He wasn't the first to import foreign players, but as with so much of what he did, he established a clear trend.

The detrimental impact of this on English football is that most transfer fees, which had previously been financially sustaining clubs in the lower divisions, are being channelled offshore. On the other hand, there is no doubt that the quality of football in the Premiership has improved to the point where it has become the most competitive and richest league in Europe.

I believe that this cumulative evidence supports the contention that a club's history since the Football Leagues were formed in the late 19th-century plays a crucial role in determining those clubs most likely to succeed today. My analysis of results since the Premiership was formed almost twenty years ago underlines the inherent advantage it bestows, but only if it is successfully exploited.

The addition of quality management, adequate funding, and an appropriate strategy will deliver success. The obverse is also true – the advantage can be, and in some cases has been, squandered. That is because the variable elements in my model have been mismanaged, probably because of a lack of strategic grasp by the Board, or a lack of funds, or both. Newcastle United is a classic case, with Leeds, without the same degree of inherent advantage, not far behind.

Returning to the model, **location** and **history** have combined to produce **a stadium** and **a loyal fanbase**. Those are the preconditions I set. The variables are the actions of **the owners** and **the Board**, who must agree a plan and appoint **a management team** and **Manager** capable of, and who will be delegated the responsibility for, creating and maintaining **a squad** that can deliver **the plan**. The Board must also raise **the money** to fuel the model which **the performance**, if successful, will replenish. ·

It works as shown in the diagram below.

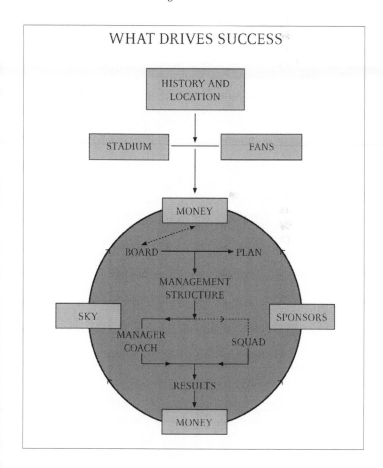

I have dealt with history in some detail, but should expand on the role that that the stadium and the fans play. They were also created by history and most have become an integral part of local culture. In Newcastle, the stadium, St James' Park, is frequently referred to as 'the third cathedral', and the city as a whole is bound up with the fortunes of the team, most visibly participated in by those who are match-going fans.

Almost 70% of the 52,000 ground capacity is taken up by season ticket holders, benefiting the club's cash flow and effectively underwriting the playing squad's payroll. Attendances have regularly been at the upper end of the league's attendance table since the ground was finally developed to the site's maximum in 2000. Only Manchester United, with 75,000, and Arsenal, with 60,000 since their move to the Emirates Stadium, have higher capacities.

I believe that where possible, a longstanding and familiar stadium should be retained, because that is as much a part of history as past results and cements the club in local culture, even if it means attendances may be constrained, providing it can house at least 35,000 fans.

Fans are even more important, for they are an integral part of the club, the team, the atmosphere, and the culture. Self-interest alone suggests that owners would do well to remember this and should regard themselves principally as stewards of an important part of local culture rather than absolute owners.

It is difficult to believe that the Premiership would have been created without the lure of money from satellite TV, which has now risen to £1 billion per annum, an average of £45 million for each club, graded by league position to give significantly more to clubs at the top.

A similar scale operates for progress to the later stages of the Champions League, which explains why clubs in serious contention in that league now often field weaker sides in domestic competitions such as the Carling Cup and even the FA Cup – unthinkable before the creation of the Premiership.

Sky, as all television, thrives on the visual appeal of an exciting occasion, and a high-profile game, with much at stake for both sides and played in a packed stadium in a gladiatorial atmosphere with a baying crowd dressed in replica strips, fits the bill perfectly.

I suggest that the optimum size for such a stadium is one that holds 35,000–45,000 fans. There is attractive incremental profit from a bigger stadium which is always full, but the cost of that for most clubs may have to be weighed carefully against the need for funds to strengthen and refresh the squad as circumstances dictate.

It is also probable that TV demands will become more pressing over time, just as the fixture list has already been varied to accommodate Sunday and Monday evening fixtures, to suit television scheduling. That is the payback all clubs should expect to face in return for the cash poured into the Premiership – there is no such thing as a free lunch.

The variables – the strategic plan, the management team, the Manager, and the playing squad – will all depend on the owner. There will not be many Roman Abramovitches around, but he has demonstrated how someone with his wealth can transform a club's future.

Since acquiring Chelsea in 2003, he has spent vast sums – incurring losses of £140 million and £80 million in the first two years of his ownership alone and greater sums since – which even he won't sustain indefinitely. He seems to be a very wealthy reincarnation of an old-style owner, doing it for the love of the game and delegating power to the team he has appointed. However, what will happen to Chelsea if and when he decides to sell? The new owner of Manchester City, Sheikh Mansour, appears to be in the same mould as Abramovitch and his choice of club could bring a rare change in the balance of power in Manchester. Alex Ferguson won't go on forever and his grip on the club's strategy is at present unchallengeable, but in the redistribution of power that will follow a change, it is possible that a revitalised City could 'wind back the clock' to pre-1948 days. Nothing is forever.

The changes in ownership at Aston Villa, Liverpool, and Manchester United have all seen Americans with an interest in sports investment buy into the Premiership as an attractive business venture while conforming more to the norm of expecting a reasonable return on, by hands-off management of, their investment. In addition, there is a familiar stress pattern building up at both Manchester United and Liverpool between fans and foreign owners.

I had hoped that Mike Ashley's interest in Newcastle United might lie somewhere between these two poles, but to date he conforms to neither any more than his predecessors did, although there is more than a hint of a changing attitude in the Tyneside air in 2010.

The Board has the responsibility for directing operations, but to do this it needs a medium to long-term plan, quite distinct from a financial budget, which is only one component of the plan.

The Board must have such a plan and also appoint a competent team, to which they can delegate the power and the funds to deliver it with confidence. Common sense? Yes, but it is where most clubs fall short. Newcastle have consistently underachieved because of the absence of a coherent plan, a failure to delegate authority, a lack of skill or care in making appointments, and persistent tinkering by the owners, or the majority shareholders, in the management processes. The result has been relegation and a club in financial meltdown, saved, perhaps temporarily, from a worse fate by Mike Ashley's timely acquisition.

On the other hand, Manchester United, Arsenal, Villa, and Everton appear to be doing most things the right way and have been doing so for some years now. The fuel for success is money, which must be injected both to start the process and to solve problems that will occur from time to time. A successful club in the top 6 should generate sufficient profits to maintain the momentum.

Fans should recognise that football is big business and must be run as such, but I also believe the best results will come only if it is run with a 'heart' and recognition of a club's central role in local culture. The required proven skill to run a big business is much more important than a local birth certificate, however difficult that is for fans to accept.

Some final thoughts on the Premiership

All businesses must take account of the context in which they operate, which changes continuously. The biggest single factor in the development of the Premiership has been the substantial and growing amount of cash injected by Sky sponsorship and coverage. It is worth considering whether or not this will continue indefinitely or at the same value? Setanta Sports, which tried to challenge Sky and caused a bidding up of values for live football matches in the process, has failed.

Will Sky ignore this or lower its bid values in future? Sky, like any other global business, may suffer from recessionary pressures and be forced to reduce its spending, regardless of other factors.

The threat of a reduction in television revenues from the broadcasters' commercial response to changes in competition is inevitable over time, but a more serious threat has arisen in 2010 through a declaration of intent by the regulator, Ofcom. It claims that Sky has distorted the market and it proposes action to reduce the company's hold on live broadcasts of Premiership matches. It is too early to say what will happen, but any change will almost certainly have the effect of reducing the rights payments made to clubs.

If nothing else, these twin threats should reinforce the case for strong financial management and meticulous forward planning.

The real question, if this was to happen, is would it affect clubs' ability to buy foreign players and if so, could this change the balance of power at the top of the Premiership? Is this why Arsenal have been so shrewd and successful in finding talent on the less expensive African continent?

Of greater potential impact is the question of whether or not an unrestricted ability to buy foreign players is damaging the prospects of the England national team? If this is so, it could cause the FA to impose some arbitrary limit on the number of foreign players any club could have on its books, or which it can field in any one game.

The spectre that Chelsea created in 1999 by fielding an 11 without one British-born player still lingers, but has never been repeated. Money values may decide this without intervention by authorities if the current decline in the exchange rate of the pound persists.

It has often been said that with the same four teams camped in the top four positions, swapping places only with each other, the Premiership has become boring and must be changed.

I would respond by asking if anyone who believes this has ever seen such quality of football played so consistently before. I have been watching the game at the highest level for over sixty years, and I haven't.

When some other Premiership clubs get their act together, there will be more variation, but it will still be within a small group of, say, twelve teams. It is hardly coincidental that English clubs are now more successful than ever before in Europe and that is the most powerful argument I can marshal in support of my plea to 'leave well alone'.

The recent grip of the top four Premiership clubs on the UEFA Champions League has not gone unnoticed by UEFA, who are actively lobbying to enforce financial restrictions on all UEFA clubs. Its efforts are really aimed at the two Champions League powerhouses, England and Spain. The essence of President of UEFA Michel Platini's case is that financial profligacy can and does destroy clubs in some cases, and distorts competition in others.

I recognise the first condition and the evidence on pages 135–37 of increasing cases of insolvency caused by inappropriate aspirations in some clubs and their fans is better dealt with by the FA as the governing body requiring the publication of annual accounts, including mandatory adherence to established standards of corporate governance.

The governing bodies of the Premiership and the Football Association can reduce risk and banish European interference by taking this seriously, which they have not hitherto done.

The supremacy of English clubs in European competitions is driven by the simple fact that the Premiership's top clubs have such strong squads, and that has been achieved by their ability to attract the best players in Europe. Yes, that poses the risk of financial profligacy addressed above, but alongside the failures of Leeds and Newcastle – both badly run and financially drained – there are the examples of Chelsea and Manchester City – where the owners are seeking to build a club and not extract financial rewards – or Manchester United and Arsenal – where management skills have been applied to all aspects of the club both on and off the field.

We know that investment in transfer fees and the payroll of the playing staff lies at the root of profligacy, but we could reduce those pressures by the simple expedient of capping the number of non-British players a club can field in any game to (for example) four. They can sign twenty if they wish, but only the specified number could play in the 90+ minutes of any match.

This could have several benefits. It would make more clubs look internally for talent and would redirect transfer cash within other UK leagues, stimulating the earlier development of homegrown talent. It could lead to an increased investment in football academies, and both could gradually lead to an improvement in the England team and its performances.

Inevitably, it would also siphon off some, not all, of the pressure on many Premiership clubs' finances.

The greatest threat to stability probably comes from the self-interest of those clubs that recognise the inevitability of being perpetual 'also rans' in the lower reaches of the Premiership, which will cause them at some stage to agitate for structural changes. This will include arguments for the creation of a second tier of the Premier League, with each tier having sixteen to eighteen clubs.

It probably will include also the familiar case for the two Glasgow clubs, Celtic and Rangers, to transfer to one or other of the new Premier League divisions. These ideas, while recognising the obvious attractions of being associated with the top clubs, still do not address the cost of maintaining that relationship. It is an incontrovertible fact that many clubs already find the cost of continued membership of the Premiership financially unsustainable.

A more pragmatic solution might be to recognise that cost by setting criteria for future membership and modify the present rule of automatic relegation from, and promotion to, the Premiership. This would create a 'semi-sealed league' with clubs for example being relegated only if they were bottom for 2 successive seasons or in the last 3 positions in 2 out of any 4 seasons.

This would modify the present automatic promotion to a new two-part qualification of a place being available provided the club elect could satisfy financial requirements and other criteria.

Nothing is forever

The season that just ended produced several firsts. Chelsea as Premier League Champions became the first club to score more than 100 goals in the process. My London candidates all finished in the top four positions for the first time. The two Merseyside clubs both scored 60 goals and achieved more than 60 points, but finished outside the top 6 positions. Even more tellingly, the first nine places in the league were secured by clubs from my list of twelve 'most likely to succeed' candidates based on history, while two others were filling the automatic promotion slots in the Championship – Newcastle and West Brom – and will be in the Premiership for the 2010/11 season.

The evidence I have produced is being absorbed by a wider audience every year, which suggests life in the Premiership will get much tougher for clubs that are badly run. After all, that's part of the reason Newcastle has suffered, since a strategy based on such evidence was rejected by Freddy Shepherd more than a decade ago.

22

The Premiership –
Cause for Concern, and
a Need for Action

I have a natural aversion to attempts to limit competition artificially and the alternatives I suggested in the previous chapter are preferable to UEFA's. However, we do need to reduce the expectations of fans, as well as those of self-interested owners and players. Above all, we should seek to make this 'beautiful game' synonymous with fairness and the pursuit of excellence, legally and openly.

I deliberately included some brief references to the growth of the game in Victorian times because this is the game we exported to the rest of the world and led to football leagues being created in all corners of it, and to a World Cup competition less than fifty years later. The challenge is to remember our place in history and our responsibilities without becoming a prisoner of that history. In my lifetime, England, post-war, travelled to Portugal and beat the national team 10-0. Today, Ronaldo and Messi, a Portuguese and an Argentine, have been publicly recognised as the world's best players in successive years.

Whether others accept it or not, we still set an example for the rest of the world to emulate and interpret. The Premiership and television have been instrumental in perpetuating that through global broadcasting of live games. Yet there are some worrying elements of the game in England which must be addressed and I intend to do no more than list these under three broad headings. This is my diagnosis of problems which are potentially seriously damaging if ignored and my principal concerns are set out below. I do not offer solutions; that is for others with the power to implement.

Who guards the guardians?

The guardians are nominally the owners and/or the boards of clubs, most of which have obligations, because they are incorporated and must meet the requirements of the Companies Act. As such, they should have adequate procedures in place to ensure that basic standards of care are exercised towards creditors, which includes season ticket holders and players as well as banks. In addition, they are required to submit annual accounts, audited by a professionally qualified accountant, to Companies House within a specified period. For clubs with a listing on the London Stock Exchange, there are more onerous obligations which carry with them the threat of sanctions for noncompliance. However, my experience at Newcastle United is that this does not work and poor corporate governance is not curbed or even challenged – hence my rhetorical question above, the answer to which must be football's governing bodies, the Football Association and the Premier League, whose chairmen may dominate the FA Football Committee. The Premier League chairmen's approach may be too self-interested, while the FA's inability to retain a chief executive for more than a few months suggests that the guardian of the guardians has neither the power nor the desire to interfere with the status quo. This is the principal cause for concern, because without clear rules and workable sanctions, it is impossible to achieve good governance standards. Good governance will not guarantee success, but abandonment of it will guarantee failure, as we have seen.

Dealing with actions which bring the game into disrepute

This is not restricted to any one party – club owners, directors, managers, players, agents, match officials, or fans – I include them all. Judged by recent events, no group is blameless. Some of the ills have been attributable to one or more parties allegedly colluding in improper practices and some of these allegations have been so serious as to warrant police investigation. In the most recent cases where managers, agents, and club officials were arrested, questioned, and cautioned, no action seems to have been taken against the suspects. If that is the conclusion, those suspected should be publicly vindicated and the causes of suspicion declared unfounded. Given the high-profile undercover investigations by agencies such as the BBC *Panorama* team, it is surely worthy of FA comment or clarification. Recent police enquiries have included suspected bribery and corruption, involving managers, players, and agents, and assault charges against players.

Yet I am unaware of the FA, the Premier League, or any club restating or introducing rules to deal with these issues on a preventative basis. Currently, there are financial limits to the action that any club can take against a player guilty of serious misconduct, which are wholly inappropriate given the level of today's players' salaries.

In truth, despite evidence of players' misconduct, encompassing physical and sexual assault, serious gambling indebtedness, drug abuse, and physical violence on the field, managers and their clubs appear reluctant to take a firm stance or publicly condemn them, because of the deemed value of the player. It is a practice that not only sets a bad example to others but is doomed to be self-defeating in the long run. Action should be taken to stamp out bad behaviour.

One change that requires no more than the enforcement of good governance principles, as adopted by businesses, would be to outlaw direct employment of football agencies or individual agents by any club, and to forbid all managers from engaging in dealings with an agency in which a member of his own family is employed.

Respect

I see this issue as distinct from bringing the game into disrepute, but it is related to it and again I believe that there are many guilty parties, including fans. But I start, as always, with those who govern the game and have national or local responsibilities. Their responsibility for the way the game is played must start with respect for the fans, who have sustained the professional game since its formation. Without them, as a vital ingredient of the game, whether seen live or televised, professional football would not have developed to be the world's most-watched sport. Today, most other businesses understand that, and frequently make their attitudes known with explicit statements of social responsibility principles. Football should follow the same course, recognising that most clubs, certainly the largest and most successful, have obligations to the local community as a whole. Fans and the club are an integral part of local culture. Fans deserve to be recognised and consulted, and their views heeded.

However, fans too must respond by improving their behaviour, particularly on match days, at home or away, and in areas surrounding the ground as well as in the town or city centre. Consideration towards others and the abandonment of obscene language is overdue, as are racist chants and the abuse of match officials.

Fans should be more conscious of the example they set to younger people by their behaviour at games. So, too, should managers, as the conduct of many is frequently unacceptable. The sight of highly paid managers gesticulating angrily at the fourth official while mouthing obscenities is appalling and unnecessary.

However, the most important issue for fans to address is their duty to the club. Football has become big business and the top clubs must run it as such if they are to bring sustainable success.

Fans' expectations should reflect the reality that no club can win everything every year and for some there should be acceptance that a sustainable place in the Premiership is beyond them. For all, there should be recognition that the criteria for success should be adjusted to match reality and that in the long run, playing exciting and attractive attacking football consistently is preferable to 'silverware', although that may be the result if not the sole objective. As owners and investors have found out, in the life of the Premiership, it requires a lot of money to participate in it, and the return is more likely to be in increased pleasure than financial gain. It is difficult, if not impossible, to build a credible case for investment in a top football club and to achieve competitive returns on that investment. Some of the more extravagant claims by supporters' groups seeking to run clubs show no understanding of this.

Introducing technology to improve decision-making on the pitch

The role and responsibilities of match officials have changed as the pace of the game has become faster, the standard of players' self-discipline has declined, and the 'cost' of refereeing errors has soared. Refereeing standards have undoubtedly improved, but officials are still exposed by TV replays as having made incorrect decisions, sometimes having been duped by players feigning injury or unfair tackles.

'You must learn to take the rough with the smooth' is no longer an appropriate response when tens, sometimes hundreds of thousands, and occasionally millions of pounds, rest on the decision. If the technology is good enough to be used to make TV more exciting, why can't it be used to assist referees at crucial moments in a game? When penalties are awarded, for instance, and there is a natural break in play to consult a fourth official. It could and should be used and to argue otherwise is to deny the wisdom and foresight other sports, such as rugby and tennis, have shown.

What next?

Whatever happens, whether in response to the issues I have raised here or through some other unforeseen pressures, the way the game is organised and run will affect millions of people. It deserves better standards of management and control. It is infinitely better if those changes are self-imposed before they are enforced. The social and economic context of our lives will bring its own pressures to bear, as it has done since the Football Leagues were formed in the late Victorian period. But who will be big and brave enough to start the ball rolling?

23

Are the Criteria for Success Valid? The Evidence of 2010–12

The chapter setting out my specified criteria for success in the Premiership is included unchanged in this edition as Chapter 21. The last 2 seasons however now offer an ideal opportunity to test some of my criteria and some of the forecasts I made in that 2010 edition against these results. Similarly my choice of club, Newcastle United, also provides a base to test what happened at club level – a perspective that enables owner, Board and manager to assess their own progress against whatever strategy they collectively chose to pursue.

The criteria I set out in detail and support with a chart, are divided into two main groups broadly those which are 'fixed' – having been determined by history, location, stadium and fans – and those which are 'variable' such as the ownership/management functions, the playing squad and the financial strength of the club. What surprises many people, sadly including some owners and managers as well as fans, is the predictability of that 'fixed' group of factors. But examination of records since the creation of the Football Leagues in the nineteenth century illustrates that the power base has shrunk with the mutation of the First Division into the Premiership rather than undergone a marked shift. Thus historically successful, famous, well-supported clubs in major cities have survived and in the main prospered whilst those with historically comparable success records in smaller cities have not achieved similar status, nor in my view are they ever likely to do so again.

To translate that assessment, when Top division results (First Division + Premiership) are compared to those for the Premier League only, there is a remarkable symmetry. For all results it is 1 Liverpool, 2 Arsenal, 3 Everton, 4 Manchester United, 5 Aston Villa, 6 Chelsea, 7 Tottenham, 8 Manchester City, 9 Newcastle and 10 Sunderland whereas Premier League only ranks them 1 Manchester United, 2 Arsenal, 3 Chelsea, 4 Liverpool, 5 Aston Villa, 6 Tottenham, 7 Everton, 8 Newcastle, 9 Blackburn Rovers and 10 Manchester City.

Neither Blackburn nor Sunderland appears in both tables and Blackburn have been relegated along with Bolton and Wolverhampton in 2012. All three of the relegated teams have had long periods of success with Blackburn winning the Premiership title as recently as 1994/95. Yet, in my view, none of the three were secure in the Premiership because of a combination of financial, attendance and location factors. Blackburn's successful history was becoming a fond memory when the Premiership was created in 1992/93 season. By a quirk of fate they gained promotion to the First Division as it transformed into the Premiership, by finishing 6th in the old Division 2 and winning the play off with Derby, Leicester and Cambridge to join Ipswich and Middlesbrough. All of those clubs have since been relegated yet Blackburn prospered at first finishing 4th, 2nd and 1st before being relegated again in 1998/99.

The most notable underperformers in the last ten years by the All Time Top Division test are Aston Villa and Newcastle. Unlike the three relegated teams, these two clubs satisfy the criteria of history, stadium, fan base and should be in the top 6 clubs virtually every year. What they have shared however is a record of continuous managerial changes. By contrast the two most successful Premiership clubs, Manchester United and Arsenal, demonstrate the advantage of having a stable experienced management team who can lessen the shock of unwanted departures from their squad by the constant recruitment and development of younger players. The two clubs I referred to in the first edition of being most likely to disturb the top four were Manchester City and Everton, by displacing their neighbours Manchester United and Liverpool for the first time in years. Both achieved that in the 2011/12 season, Everton achieved it more gradually whereas Manchester City's progression from 11th to 5th, 3rd and 1st in successive seasons has been powered by vast sums of money and a wise choice of manager. Sustainability is the key issue here, as indeed it is at Chelsea despite the fact that success brings very substantial rewards.

Whilst the contribution to income of gate receipts has declined in importance as TV and other media income has soared, it is still important and is a reliable yardstick to the prospects individual clubs have for continuous membership of the Premier League. Attendances are now stable and irrespective of the constituent clubs average about 35,000 per game per week throughout the season. There is however a wide range around this number from Manchester United's 75,000, Arsenal's 60,000 and Newcastle's 50,000 to the lower half of the attendance table. It is this which correlates to financial stability and a continuing presence in the Premiership. In the last ten years clubs which fall below an average home gate of 30,000 have been West Ham four times in either 10th or 11th place, Sheffield United once in 11th, Derby once in 12th, Middlesbrough once in 13th and Southampton three times in 11th, 12th and 14th. None of these clubs have been able to enjoy a prolonged stay in the Premiership – and there are many clubs with lower attendances below those quoted. There is a real danger that such clubs will face financial difficulties in pursuit of their Premiership ambitions. Given this picture it is simply unthinkable that Newcastle United or Aston Villa should be regularly in the lower half of the table yet that is where Newcastle have finished as often as they have been in the top half. As my first edition of this book made clear the reasons for Newcastle's dismal record are clear – a trampling on the history and fan base by the owners who also made some disastrous managerial appointments and dismissals. The reason for Aston Villa's poor record may be another case of an overseas owner seeking to treat it as a conventional investment vehicle allied to another case of frequent managerial changes.

The 60-goal target I first discussed with the then owners of Newcastle in 1997/98 still holds good and remains the simplest way to achieve a top 4/6 place. That is remarkable because two new goal-scoring records have been achieved in the last three years. Last season the total number of Premiership goals scored in all matches reached 1066 and in 2009/10 Chelsea scored over 100 goals in a season for the first time. Whilst most of the heavy spending in recent years has been to acquire strikers, usually from abroad, that spending has been concentrated in the top half of the table.

Whilst the 60-goal criterion appears to have been widely recognised or adopted by the top clubs, the risks that many clubs face in the lower reaches of the Premiership are less well recognised. It is true that the safety level to avoid relegation is seen as 40 points and that is validated by the fact that since 2000 only one club with more than 40 points has been relegated. But if 60 points will usually ensure a top 6 place and 40 virtually guarantees 17th place or better, that still means eleven clubs will achieve between 40 and 60 points and survive. Every club has a poor run of form at some stage in the season and this means that eleven clubs can experience a season of continuous pressure such as QPR, an obvious relegation candidate, experienced last season. The evidence suggests that this probability does not receive adequate consideration before substantial investment is made. The relegation places most seasons are filled, as are the replacement clubs promoted in the same season, principally by a rotating list of the same clubs I listed in the first edition. In 2010/11 the relegated clubs were Birmingham, Blackpool and

West Ham and in 2011/12 Bolton, Blackburn and Wolverhampton while the replacement promoted clubs were in 2010/11 QPR, Norwich and Swansea and in 2011/12 Reading, Southampton and West Ham. This fact reinforces my belief that insolvency and other financial difficulties are associated more with clubs seeking to fulfil unrealistic ambitions rather than through investment by long time residents of the Premiership seeking to maintain or regain their competitive edge.

I doubt if the immediate future will bring dramatic changes to the behaviour of owners, managers, players or fans – some will simply be more soundly reasoned than others. Whatever lies ahead here's to many more years of football involvement and watching.

Newcastle United in the Premier League (Performance Review 1993–2012)

Season	Position	Games P	W	D	L	Goals F	A	GD	Pts
2011/12	5	38	19	8	11	56	51	+5	65
2010/11	12	38	11	13	14	56	57	-1	46
2009/10	*Newcastle in Coca-Cola Championship*								
	1	46	30	12	4	90	35	+55	102
2008/09	18	38	7	13	18	40	59	-19	34
2007/08	12	38	11	10	17	45	65	-20	43
2006/07	13	38	11	10	17	38	47	-9	43
2005/06	7	38	17	7	14	47	42	+5	58
2004/05	14	38	10	14	14	47	57	-10	44
2003/04	5	38	13	17	8	52	40	+12	56
2002/03	3	38	21	6	11	63	48	+15	69
2001/02	4	38	21	8	9	74	52	+22	71
2000/01	11	38	14	9	15	44	50	-6	51
1999/00	11	38	14	10	14	63	54	+9	52
1998/99	13	38	11	13	14	48	54	-6	46
1997/98	13	38	11	11	16	35	44	-9	44
1996/97	2	38	19	11	8	73	40	+33	68
1995/96	2	38	24	6	8	66	37	+29	78
1994/95	6	42	20	12	10	67	47	+20	72
1993/94	3	42	23	8	11	82	41	+41	77
1992/93	*Inaugural Season – Newcastle become First Division Champions*								
	1	46	29	9	8	92	38	+54	96
1991/92	First Division								

The Price of Failure

Year ended 31 July (30 June from 2006)	2007 £	2006 £	2005 £	2004 £	200 £
WF Shepherd					
Salary/fees	500,000	458,333	500,000	500,000	41€
Taxable benefits	3,617	3,020	2,954	3,145	
Bonus/compensation for loss of office	1,007,234			164,000	25€
Money purchase pension contributions	50,000	45,833	50,000	50,000	
Total	1,560,851	507,186	552,954	717,145	66€
No. shares held	37,278,505	37,278,505	34,355,318	32,335,318	32,33€
Dividend	0	0	1,054,708	992,694	99€
Total take	1,560,851	507,186	1,607,662	1,709,839	1,66
No. share sold	37,278,505				
Price per share (pence)	101.0				
Value	37,651,290				
Total take (incl. share sales)	39,212,141	507,186	1,607,662	1,709,839	1,66
DS Hall					
Salary/fees	448,654	412,500	450,000	450,000	36€
Taxable benefits	1,136	1,046	951	465	
Bonus/compensation for loss of office	1,173,783			140,000	22
Money purchase pension contributions	44,865	41,250	45,000	45,000	
Total	1,668,438	454,796	495,951	635,465	59
No. shares held	55,342,223	55,342,223	52,937,065	52,937,065	57,32€
Dividend	0	0	1,625,168	1,625,168	1,75€
Total take	1,668,438	454,796	2,121,119	2,260,633	2,35€
No. share sold	55,342,223			4,388,887	
Price per share (pence)	100.0			27.1	
Value	55,342,223			1,189,388	
Total take (incl. share sales)	57,010,661	454,796	2,121,119	3,450,021	2,35€
NU PLC					
Dividend declared	0.00p	0.00p	3.07p	3.07	
Total Hall/Shepherd family take	96,222,802	961,982	3,728,781	5,159,861	4,01

NOTES:

1999 - DSH's dividend was taken in shares

1996 - DSH Salary/fees includes a sum of £836,803 paid to Sir JH

2002 - Note shares sold as a result of buy back

Additional payments of £6.5m were made by Newcastle United PLC to DHS between 1996 and 2007 in related party transactions

Additional payments of £2.007m were made by Newcastle United PLC to WFS between 1996 and 2007 in related party transactions

Source: Newcastle United Annual Accounts and announcements via the London Stock Exchamge

2	2001 £	2000 £	1999 £	1998 £	1997 £	1996 £	TOTAL
0,000	232,868	75,000	23,533	22,622	14,583	750,000	3,823,606
1,639					2,747		29,375
0,000							1,671,234
							195,833
1,639	232,868	75,000	23,533	22,622	17,330	750,000	5,720,048
5,318	30,580,333	11,842,819	11,619,370	11,619,370	11,169,370	10,428,630	
1,994	938,816	312,650	204,501	204,501	5,585	0	5,668,144
3,633	1,171,684	387,650	228,034	227,123	22,915	750,000	11,388,192
							37,651,290
3,633	1,171,684	387,650	228,034	227,123	22,915	750,000	49,039,482
2,762	110,000	41,667	35,000	22,622	14,583	1,630,415	4,294,870
1,495					336		15,429
0,000							1,738,783
							176,115
4,257	110,000	41,667	35,000	22,622	14,919	1,630,415	6,225,197
5,952	69,447,165	69,477,165	73,447,610	82,347,610	82,797,610	8,187,687	
9,907	2,132,028	1,834,197	1,292,678	1,449,318	41,399	0	13,519,769
4,164	2,242,028	1,875,864	1,327,678	1,471,940	56,318	1,630,415	19,744,966
1,213	12,121,213		4,729,260	9,000,000			
27.1			111.7	111.7			
4,849			5,282,583	10,053,000			75,152,044
9,012	2,242,028	1,875,864	6,610,261	11,524,940	56,318	1,630,415	94,897,010
3.07p	3.07p	2.64p	1.76p	1.76p	0.05p	0.00p	
2,646	3,413,712	2,263,515	6,838,295	11,752,063	79,232	2,380,415	143,936,492

Acknowledgements

A number of my football friends deserve special thanks for their direct contributions to this book, whether it was through research, guidance, or criticism. I hope those whose names do not appear will understand that it is impossible to include everyone.

Martin Purvis compiled Appendix II and directed me to various reference sources; John Josephs, a former Board colleague at St James' Park, Michael Pescod, Charles Rose, and David Groves all read the draft book and offered helpful criticism and support. Freddie Fletcher, another former colleague, knew of my opinions, which we discussed over many happy hours, often at matches at St James' Park. The extract from the Wembley Programme of April 2000 has been reproduced by kind permission of the Football Association. The cover photograph is courtesy of Getty Images.

My late friend Sir Bobby Robson would have contributed a foreword had he survived the completion of the book. He and I shared strong and similar views about the game and the professional behaviour of those in it.

All of my efforts would have been wasted but for the patience and skill which my colleague Patricia Keaveny applied to transforming drafts, notes, and drawings into a readable manuscript. My wife Ronda has again been supportive throughout the long process.

Finally I am grateful to Alan Sutton and Amberley Publishing for their confidence in so readily agreeing to publish *Newcastle United: The Day the Promises Had to Stop.*

I hope all of their collective efforts will be rewarded by its success.

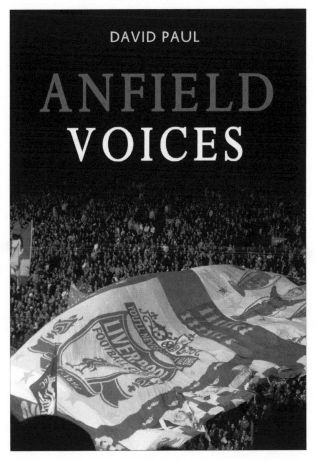

Anfield Voices
David Paul

Anfield Voices brings together a wonderful collection of
photographs, fond memories and fascinating anecdotes recalling
the good, and not so good, times of one of England's oldest, most
prestigious and most successful football teams.

978 1 4456 0195 3
128 pages, 97 b&w illustrations

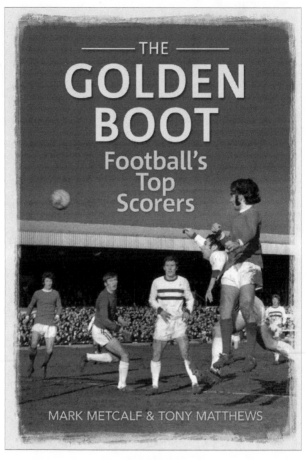

The Golden Boot
Football's Top Scorers
Mark Metcalf *&* Tony Matthews

The first history of the Golden Boot – from 1888 to the present day.

978 1 4456 0532 6
256 pages, illustrated throughout

Available from all good bookshops or order direct
from our website www.amberleybooks.com